Sirah of Our Prophet ﷺ

A MERCY TO MANKIND

D1304824

TEXTBOOK
GRADE 6

Abidullah Ghazi & Tasneema Ghazi

Part of a Comprehensive and Systematic Program of Islamic Studies

A Textbook for the program of *Sirah*

**Mercy To Mankind:
Madinah Period**

Chief Program Editors
Dr. Abidullah Ghazi
(Ph.D., Study of Religion
Harvard University)

Dr. Tasneema Ghazi
(Ph.D., Curriculum-Reading
University of Minnesota)

Editing
Huseyin Abiva
Dilshad Ali

Religious Editors
Dr. Muzzamil Siddiqi
Sh. Saeed Dabbas
Sh. Muhammad Khalidi

Maps
Huseyin Abiva

Design and Layout
Yousef Ouri

Revised Expanded Edition, 2006
Second Printing, 2008
Third Printing, 2012
Fourth Printing, 2017
Fifth Printing, 2020
Printed in Turkey
Copyright © 1991, IQRA' International
Educational Foundation.
All Rights Reserved

IQRA' International Educational Foundation

**7450 Skokie Blvd., Skokie, IL 60077
Tel: 847-673-4072 Fax: 847-673-4095**

Website:www.iqra.org

LCCN:94-65596
ISBN # 1-56316-156-7

IQRA's Note

It is with great happiness that we present this new, completely revised and expanded edition of IQRA's popular textbook, Mercy to Mankind Madinah Period. This textbook was first published in 1982 has since ran into numerous reprintings.

We are thankful to Allah ﷻ for His guidance and our *ansar* and supporters for their assistance in the completion of this valuable work. This book is nothing less than the product of the love and devotion that we hold for our beloved Prophet Muhammad ﷺ. It is our deepest desire that all of our readers, no matter what the age, will enjoy the blessings of reading this *Sirah*, the life story of the Prophet ﷺ.

These days it is important that we refresh ourselves with the significance of the *Sirah* and strive to implement it as a model for our own lives.

This revised and expanded edition of Mercy to Mankind Madinah Period includes following distinctive features:

1. Twelve new lessons dealing with the noble personality of Rasulullah ﷺ and some of his Ahadith are added.
2. A focal point now introduces each lesson under the heading "Looking Ahead".
3. Students are challenged to use critical thinking skills during their study of the text.
4. Qur'anic teachings are integrated into each lesson.
5. Geography skills are incorporated into the text by means of attractive and topographically accurate maps of the many places of historical importance in the *Sirah*.
6. The book has been attractively designed and printed in full color.

We pray that this work, Mercy to Mankind Madinah Period, will instill feelings of love and devotion for the Noble Prophet ﷺ into the hearts and minds of our readers, encouraging them to follow his *Sunnah* with both right thoughts and right actions.

Dr. Abidullah Ghazi
Executive Director
IQRA' International Educational Foundation
Safar 28, 1426/March 31, 2006

About the Book
The following presents the highlights of this textbook

Looking Ahead
- This boxed feature gets the student ready to take on each lesson by providing a brief synopsis of its content.

Side Bars and Critical Thinking Skills
- These features enhance the core material of the text by providing the student with multi-layered contextualization and wider perspectives on the subject matter.

Illustrations and Maps
- Full color illustrations with detailed and geographically accurate maps will encourage students to take deeper appreciation of the topic being discussed.

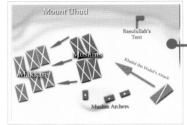

The Battle of Uhud

Words to Know
- This feature introduces the new words and Islamic vocabulary used in the lesson.

Qur'an/Hadith
- Connection: Each lesson concludes with either a single Ayah or Hadith intended to encapsulate the transcendental relevance of the lesson's message beyond the historical event.

Table of Contents

The cost of printing this book was made possible through a donation from the family of the late Ashraf Sultan with the intention of *Isal Ath-Thawab* (إيصال الثواب) on her soul, so please remember her in your *Du'a'*.

Rasulullah ﷺ is Welcomed to Madinah

Lesson 1

Looking Ahead

Rasulullah ﷺ was finally able to find protection in Madinah. We will see the great welcome he was given by the people of Madinah.

Rasulullah's journey from Makkah to Madinah took about two weeks. The Prophet Muhammad ﷺ, his beloved companion Abu Bakr ﷺ, and a servant traveled through the desert on their camels. After many days the three men reached a little village just outside Madinah named Quba. The people of Quba were anxiously waiting for them.

Rasulullah ﷺ and Abu Bakr ﷺ stayed in Quba for a few days to rest from their long journey. While they were there they built a small *masjid* called *Masjid Quba.* In doing this Rasulullah ﷺ showed that wherever Muslims go to live they must first build a *masjid*. A few days later Rasulullah ﷺ and Abu Bakr ﷺ set out for Madinah. By that time 'Ali ﷺ arrived from Makkah to join them.

It was a festive day in Madinah when the Prophet Muhammad ﷺ arrived. All the men, women, and children of the city came out to greet him. They were very happy to see Rasulullah ﷺ. They met him with cries of "Welcome! O Messenger of Allah! Welcome!"

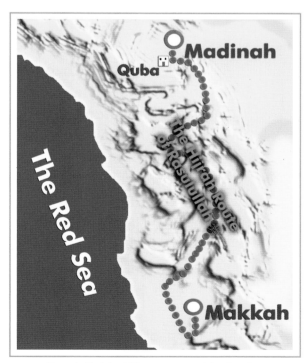

Rasulullah's *Hijra* route to Madinah

All the children greeted him with a beautiful song:

"The full moon rises from the Valley of Wada'
To shine on us all!
You gave us the Light of Your faith,
We thank you O Allah!"

The children ran to Rasulullah ﷺ. He stopped to hug them. "Do you love me children?" he asked. "Yes! We love you!" said the children. Rasulullah ﷺ smiled and replied, "I love all of you too!"

Everyone loved Rasulullah ﷺ and every family wanted him to stay with them. It would be a great honor and blessing to be the Prophet's host.

Rasulullah ﷺ saw how happy the people were. He did not want to disappoint anyone by picking a house to stay in. So he decided to let his camel Qaswa choose where he would stay. "Where my camel stops, that's where I shall sleep," he said to everyone.

The people watched as Qaswa walked through the streets of Madinah. Finally it stopped in front of the house of a man named Abu Ayyub ﷺ. Abu Ayyub ﷺ and his wife were very happy. They offered their house to Rasulullah ﷺ and his companions. Rasulullah ﷺ accepted their invitation. He stayed in Abu Ayyub's house until his own house was built. Because Abu Ayyub helped Rasulullah ﷺ he became known throughout history as Abu Ayyub al-Ansari, Abu Ayyub "the Helper."

Abu Ayyub al-Ansari ﷺ
After he embraced Islam, Abu Ayyub ﷺ served Islam faithfully. He had the honor of carrying the Prophet's flags in all the battles against the Makkans. Many years later, when he was in his 80's, Abu Ayyub ﷺ took part in the siege of Constantinople. He died outside the walls and his grave in Turkey is still visited by thousands of the faithful to this day.

Most of the people living in Madinah accepted Islam. However some people only pretended to be Muslims while, in fact, they were against Islam. These people were called *Munafiqun* (hypocrites). A *munafiq* is someone who says one thing but does something else. The *Munafiqun* did not like Rasulullah ﷺ living in Madinah. They soon began to help the Makkan *Kuffar*.

WE HAVE LEARNED
● The people of Madinah welcomed Prophet Muhammad ﷺ.
● Rasulullah ﷺ stayed in the house of Abu Ayyub al-Ansari ﷺ.

WORDS TO KNOW
Festive, *Munafiqun,* Quba

HADITH CONNECTION
The word *"Ansar"* means "Helper". The Prophet Muhammad ﷺ called the Muslims of Madinah *"Ansar"* because they helped the Muslims from Makkah. Rasulullah ﷺ said about these people:

"The *Ansar* are my family and my trusted friends. People will increase in number while they will decrease, so appreciate the deeds of the *Ansar* who do good and overlook their faults."
(*Sahih Muslim*)

The *masjid* and grave of Abu Ayyub al-Ansari ﷺ in Istanbul, Turkey

The Masjid An-Nabi is Built

Looking Ahead

A *masjid* is for more than making *salat*, the five daily prayers. As you read this lesson find how the early Muslims used this special place.

After he arrived in Madinah, Rasulullah ﷺ bought a piece of land. This land was in front of the house of Abu Ayyub al-Ansari ﷺ. The Muslims started building a *masjid* on this land. This way Rasulullah ﷺ showed how important it is for Muslims to build *masjid* wherever they live. Rasulullah ﷺ said, "Whoever builds a *masjid*, Allah will reward him with a palace in Paradise."

All the *Muhajirun* and *Ansar* worked hard to build the *masjid*. Rasulullah ﷺ himself worked day and night along with them. Many people did not want the Prophet to work at all. "You are our leader and Allah's Prophet," they said. "We want you to rest and relax!"

"The leader of the people," Rasulullah ﷺ answered, "must be their servant." He set an example that leaders should be the helpers of humankind. In fact they should work even harder than others.

The Muslims were happy when the *masjid* was finally built. They started making *salat* in the *masjid* five times a day. The people called this place the *Masjid an-Nabi*, which means "The Prophet's Mosque."

On one side of the *Masjid an-Nabi* rooms were built for Rasulullah ﷺ and his family to live in. This made it easy for people to reach Rasulullah ﷺ. People visited him every day at the time of *salat*. After *Fajr* prayer, he would sit with the men and teach them. After *Maghrib* prayer, the women would come and learn.

Rasulullah ﷺ was always available for those who came to see him. He showed us that those who want to serve others and teach Islam

THINK ABOUT IT!

Why do you think every Muslim community should have a masjid?

should live among the people. Muslims must participate in helping their communities. They should try to work together with their neighbors, both Muslims and non-Muslims, to spread goodness and peace.

In the *Masjid an-Nabi* there was a long and wide bench called the *Suffah*. Many *Sahabah* who came from the outside and had no families in Madinah stayed there. These people were called the *Ashab as-Suffah*, the People of the Bench. They were full-time students in the first "University of Islam" and their teacher was the Prophet ﷺ himself. Rasulullah ﷺ had special love for *Ashab as-Suffah*. He wanted them to stay close to him.

When Rasulullah ﷺ passed away, he was buried in the room of his wife A'isha ﷺ. This room was next to the *Masjid an-Nabi*. Several years later his two friends, Abu Bakr and 'Umar ﷺ, were buried next to him.

Nowadays the *Masjid an-Nabi* is very, very big. Tens of thousands of people go there every year to make *salat*. They go to the grave of Rasulullah ﷺ to give him *Salam* and to recite *Salawat* to him. People also go to the graves of his *Sahabah* to send them greetings of peace.

> ## Three Moons
> There is a story related by 'A'isha ﷺ that she once had a dream in which she saw three moons setting into her room. When Rasulullah ﷺ passed away, 'A'isha's father, Abu Bakr ﷺ, told her that the first moon that set was Rasulullah ﷺ. Then, when Abu Bakr ﷺ passed away and was buried beside his beloved friend, 'A'ishah knew that her father was the second moon and that 'Umar ﷺ would soon be the third.

WE HAVE LEARNED

- Rasulullah ﷺ helped build *Masjid an-Nabi*.
- After the *Masjid an-Nabi* was built, the Muslims prayed there five times a day.
- The Prophet ﷺ and his family lived in rooms on one side of the *Masjid an-Nabi*.

WORDS TO KNOW

Ashab as-Suffah, Bench, *Masjid an-Nabi*, *Salat*

QUR'AN CONNECTION

Allah says in the Qur'an about those who build and visit the *masjid*:

إِنَّمَا يَعْمُرُ مَسَٰجِدَ ٱللَّهِ مَنْ ءَامَنَ بِٱللَّهِ وَٱلْيَوْمِ ٱلْءَاخِرِ وَأَقَامَ ٱلصَّلَوٰةَ وَءَاتَى ٱلزَّكَوٰةَ وَلَمْ يَخْشَ إِلَّا ٱللَّهَ فَعَسَىٰ أُو۟لَٰٓئِكَ أَن يَكُونُوا۟ مِنَ ٱلْمُهْتَدِينَ ﴿١٨﴾

*"Only he will build and visit Allah's Masjid who believes in Allah
and the Day of Judgment, who observes salat, pays zakat,
and does not fear anyone except Allah. It is they who are expected
to be on true guidance"*

(*at-Tawbah* 9:18)

The Brotherhood of the *Muhajirun* and *Ansar*

Looking Ahead

The Muslims are one Family, one *ummah*. How did Rasulullah ﷺ ask the people of Madinah and Makkah to show their togetherness?

The *Muhajirun* left everything they owned behind in Makkah, but the Muslims of Madinah helped them out. They took the *Muhajirun* in as their guests and shared food and money with them. Because of this, they were called the *Ansar* or "Helpers." Allah ﷻ awarded them with this name in the Qur'an. The *Ansar* were very happy with their new title.

Soon after his arrival in Madinah, the Prophet Muhammad ﷺ called together all the *Muhajirun* and the *Ansar*. "All Muslims are brothers and sisters to each other," he said. "The *Muhajirun* have left their homes in Makkah. They gave up everything they owned for their Faith. I want each *Ansar* to accept one *Muhajir* to be his brother."

Brotherhood (*Muwakhat*)

Muwakhat was a very important step in bringing unity to the early Muslim community. The purpose of this brotherhood was not only to help the *Muhajirun* in their new environment, but to start a new community based on faith. Arab society before Islam was one that was based on tribes and clans. People could not imagine being loyal and devoted to anyone who was not of their tribe. The *Muhajirun* and *Ansar* loved each other and cared for one another as if they were one family. They worked with each other, learning from Rasulullah ﷺ. Together they helped the cause of Islam. Allah then blessed them and gave them success in the end. Had the Muslims remained divided by tribe, they certainly would not have achieved what they achieved during the lifetime of the Prophet ﷺ.

Think about those people who have suffered recently through earthquakes or tsunamis. How could you help?

The *Ansar* were ready to do everything to make the Prophet ﷺ happy. Each one of them took a *Muhajir* to be his brother. "You are our brothers in Islam," the *Ansar* said to the *Muhajirun*. "You have an equal share in everything we own. Allah will bless us and our property if we share it with you."

The *Muhajirun* were very pleased to have such kind helpers, but they took only as much as they needed. Some of them soon learned agriculture from the *Ansar* and became farmers. Others started their own businesses. The *Muhajirun* and the *Ansar* lived together like one big family. The brotherhood of the *Ansar* and the *Muhajirun* is called *the Muwakhat*.

The Muslims living in Madinah had a government of their own. Rasulullah ﷺ was their prophet, their leader, their guide, and their teacher. They met five times a day in the *Masjid an-Nabi* to pray. If there was an argument or dispute, Rasulullah ﷺ would settle it. Each day the Prophet Muhammad ﷺ taught the *Sahabah* how to come close to Allah ﷻ.

Whenever *wahi*, or revelations, came, Rasulullah ﷺ recited the *ayat* to the people. Some of them wrote down the words of the Qur'an as they came to the Prophet ﷺ while others learned them by heart.

The Muslims obeyed Rasulullah ﷺ in all matters, but he discussed many things with his *Sahabah* and often asked their advice. Allah has told Muslims to reach decisions by consultation. This way is called *shura*. In taking the advice of the *Sahabah,* the Prophet Muhammad ﷺ showed how people should decide their affairs through *shura*.

WE HAVE LEARNED

- Prophet Muhammad ﷺ asked the *Ansar* to accept the *Muhajirun* as their brothers. They shared everything they had with the *Muhajirun*.
- Rasulullah ﷺ taught us to use *shura* to make important decisions.

WORDS TO KNOW

Agriculture, Brotherhood, *Muwakhat, Shura, Wahi*

QUR'AN CONNECTION

Allah ﷻ says in the Qur'an about the brotherhood of the believers:

$$\text{إِنَّ ٱلَّذِينَ ءَامَنُواْ وَهَاجَرُواْ وَجَهَدُواْ بِأَمْوَٰلِهِمْ وَأَنفُسِهِمْ}$$
$$\text{فِى سَبِيلِ ٱللَّهِ وَٱلَّذِينَ ءَاوَواْ وَّنَصَرُواْ أُوْلَٰئِكَ بَعْضُهُمْ أَوْلِيَآءُ بَعْضٍ}$$

"Certainly those who believe and made Hijrah, and struggled with their wealth and their lives in the Way of Allah and those who gave the Muhajirun shelter and help, they are friends of each other."

(al-Anfal 8:72)

Lesson 4
A Treaty with the Jewish Tribes

Looking Ahead

Madinah was home to three tribes that followed the religion of Judaism. How do Muslims and Jews share a common heritage?

Before the coming of Islam, most of the people who lived in Madinah worshiped many gods. However, there were three large tribes that followed Judaism living near the city. The followers of the religion of Judaism are called "Jewish." They believe in One God just like the Muslims. Allah ﷻ sent many prophets to the Jewish people in the past. They followed Prophet Musa ﷺ, who had been given the *Tawrat*, which is often called the "Hebrew Bible." They also followed Prophet Dawud ﷺ, who received the *Zabur*, or "Psalms" The Qur'an calls the Jews "People of the Book" because they too received Allah's Books.

Rasulullah ﷺ hoped that these "People of the Book" who lived in Madinah would believe in his message. But most of them did not believe that Rasulullah ﷺ was really a prophet, since prophets had always come from their own tribes. So it was also hard for them to accept him.

Rasulullah ﷺ respected their decision not to follow Islam. But he still wanted peace between Muslims and the Jewish tribes. "We live in one city. We worship the same God. We are all one community," he told everyone. "We should help each other and live in peace. If we are attacked, we will defend ourselves together. We should make an agreement of peace and cooperation."

The leaders of the Jewish tribes liked the Prophet's plan. They signed a treaty with the Muslims. This agreement is called the "Charter of Madinah." It was the one of the first written treaties in history.

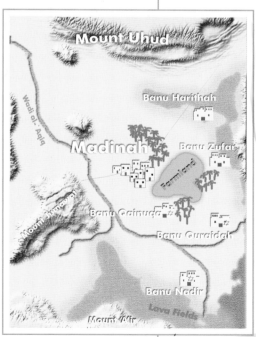

The City of Madinah

But this agreement did not last very long. Some of the Jewish chiefs became worried about what would happen to their way of life if the Muslims became too strong. So they decided, instead, to help the *Kuffar* and the *Munafiqun* against the Muslims. This worried Rasulullah ﷺ very much. He loved peace, and he wanted to live in peace with everyone.

Islam is a religion of peace, and it teaches us to live in peace with all of our fellow human beings. Rasulullah ﷺ showed us through his example that

The Charter of Madinah

- This is a document from Muhammad the Prophet about relations between those Believers from the Quraish and Yathrib and those who followed them and worked hard with them. They form one community.
- All citizens will oppose those who encourage unfairness or sin.
- Those Jewish people who ally with the Muslims will be helped and will be treated with equality.
- No Jewish person will be mistreated simply for being Jewish. The Muslims have their faith and the Jews theirs.
- The enemies of the Jewish tribes will not be helped. The enemies of the Muslims will not be helped.
- When you differ on anything you shall ask Allah and His Messenger.
- The Jewish allies will contribute towards the war when fighting alongside the Muslims.
- Those in alliance with the Jewish tribes will be given the same treatment as the Jewish tribes.
- No one in Madinah shall go to war except with the permission of the Messenger of Allah.
- The Jewish tribes are responsible for their own expenses and the Muslims theirs.
- If anyone attacks anyone who agrees to this Charter all others must come to his help.
- A person will not be made responsible for the crimes of his ally.
- The Banu Quraish and its allies will not be given protection.

Muslims must always be fair and just to everyone, Muslim and non-Muslim.

WE HAVE LEARNED
- The Jews have a special relationship with Muslims.
- Prophet Muhammad ﷺ made an agreement to live in peace with the Jewish tribes of Madinah.
- The Jewish chiefs became worried at the strength of the Muslims.

WORDS TO KNOW
Chief, People of the Book, *Tawrat, Zabur*

QUR'AN CONNECTION
Muslims have a special relationship with the People of the Book. They share the belief in One God. Allah ﷻ says in the Qur'an:

$$قُلْ يَـٰٓأَهْلَ ٱلْكِتَـٰبِ تَعَالَوْاْ إِلَىٰ$$

$$كَلِمَةٍ سَوَآءٍ بَيْنَنَا وَبَيْنَكُمْ أَلَّا نَعْبُدَ إِلَّا ٱللَّهَ$$

*"Say (O Muhammad): O People of the Book! Come to
an agreement between you and us, that we
shall not worship anyone besides Allah."*

(Ali Imran 3:64)

Lesson 5

An Alliance Against the Muslims

Looking Ahead

Even though many people were happy with Rasulullah's arrival in Madinah, there were those who were not. Read about what they did to show their displeasure.

In Madinah the number of Muslims grew very fast as every day more and more people came to Islam. However, there were many people who did not like this.

One of these people was a man named Ibn Ubai. He was one of the *Munafiqun*. Ibn Ubai was jealous of Rasulullah ﷺ, and he wanted to be the ruler of Madinah himself. He did not want people to follow Allah ﷻ and Rasulullah ﷺ. But he hid these feelings from almost everyone. He pretended to be a Muslim while in his heart he did not like Islam. Ibn Ubai sent secret messages to Makkah. The *Kuffar* made Ibn Ubai their friend. They asked him to help them defeat the Muslims.

Many of the Jewish chiefs began to worry about the Muslims too. These chiefs had many friends from among the Arab tribes, and they had a lot of influence. But as more and more people accepted Islam, their influence grew weaker. This upset them.

The *Kuffar* sent letters to the *Munafiqun* and chiefs of the three Jewish tribes to ask for help against the Muslims. The three groups decided to join together and become allies. Together they became a powerful force.

The Muslims in Madinah now found themselves in a difficult situation. There were people wanting to do them harm both inside and outside the city. The *Munafiqun* were especially dangerous. They pretended to be Muslims on the outside but secretly plotted against the

Muslim community. They came to all the meetings and gatherings. They sat with Rasulullah ﷺ, and passed on all the information they could get to their allies.

But Rasulullah ﷺ understood the intentions of those who wanted to harm the community. Even though times were growing to be unsafe, the believers had faith in Allah ﷻ and His Messenger, Muhammad Rasulullah ﷺ.

WE HAVE LEARNED
- The *Kuffar* wanted to stop the spread of Islam.
- Ibn Ubai, the leader of *Munafiqun*, became an ally of the Makkans.
- The Jewish tribes felt threatened by the Muslims' power and joined with the *Kuffar* and the *Munafiqun*.

WORDS TO KNOW
Ally, Arms, Fortresses, Hostile, Protected

QUR'AN CONNECTION
Allah ﷻ says in the Qur'an about those who will not have success,

$$إِنَّ ٱلَّذِينَ كَفَرُواْ وَصَدُّواْ عَن سَبِيلِ ٱللَّهِ وَشَاقُّواْ ٱلرَّسُولَ مِنْ بَعْدِ مَا تَبَيَّنَ لَهُمُ ٱلْهُدَىٰ لَن يَضُرُّواْ ٱللَّهَ شَيْئًا وَسَيُحْبِطُ أَعْمَٰلَهُمْ ﴿٣٢﴾$$

"Certainly those who disbelieve and who turn away from the path of Allah and fight the Prophet after guidance has been made clear to them, cannot harm Allah in any way, and Allah will make their actions unsuccessful."

(*Muhammad* 47:32)

Lesson 6

The Battle of Badr

(The 2nd year of the *Hijrah*)

Looking Ahead

Having been patient with persecution for so long, Allah gave the Muslims permission to defend themselves from those who wanted to do them harm.

The Muslims in Madinah formed one *Ummah*, or community. The *Masjid an-Nabi* was the meeting place of the *Ummah*. The Prophet Muhammad ﷺ was their leader. Every day he taught them how to worship Allah ﷻ and how to be good human beings.

Allah ﷻ began to reveal new rules and laws for the Muslims to follow. He ordered the Muslims to fast during the month of Ramadan. "*Sawm* (fasting) is done for Me," Allah ﷻ told the Prophet ﷺ, "and I will reward those who fast." How glad the Muslims were to receive this promise from Allah ﷻ!

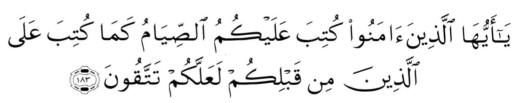

*"O you who believe, fasting has been prescribed for you
as it has been prescribed for people before you
so that you will attain Taqwa."*

(al-Baqarah, 2:183)

Fasting in Other Religious Traditions

Fasting is not only an Islamic practice, but it is a part of other religious traditions as well. Jews fast from food and drink for a 24-hour period from sundown to sundown on a day called Youm Kippour. Other Jewish fasts last only from sunrise to sunset. Christians also have different types of fasts. Many abstain from meat on the special days of Ash Wednesday and Good Friday, and traditionally abstain from meat on all Fridays in the season of Lent. Fasting in Hinduism and Buddhism is commonly practiced on New Moon days and during festivals.

But their happiness did not last long. The *Kuffar* were planning to attack the Muslims with an army. They called together their friends. They began to make preparations for war.

Two years before, the Muslims had been persecuted and finally forced to leave Makkah. During that time Allah ﷻ did not allow the Muslims to retaliate. But in Madinah the situation had changed. Allah ﷻ knew the plans of the *Kuffar*. He also knew that the Muslims were patient. Allah ﷻ now sent *wahi* to the Prophet Muhammad ﷺ ordering the Muslims to defend themselves against those who wanted to attack them.

The first battle between the Muslims and the *Kuffar* was fought at the Wells of Badr. This was a place located about 70 miles southwest of Madinah.

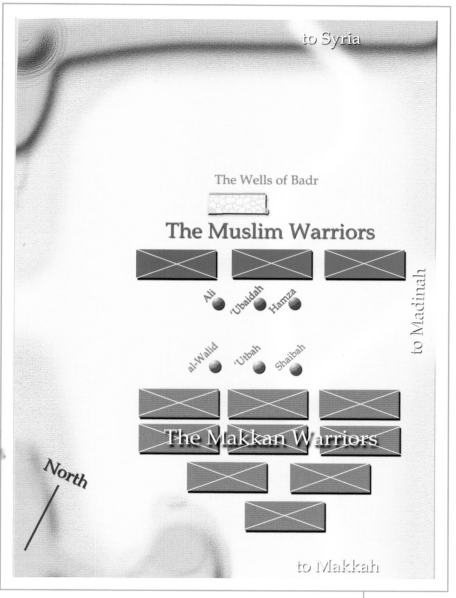

The Battlefield of Badr

Exactly 313 Muslims fought against more than 1,000 *Kuffar*. The Muslims were poor and did not have enough weapons or armor. But Allah ﷻ was with them.

The Muslims fought bravely during the battle. They were fighting against people who had persecuted them and driven them out of their homes. The Muslims were fighting to defend Islam. Even though they were outnumbered, the Muslims were not afraid. They were making *jihad* in the Way of Truth.

The word *jihad* means to struggle for the sake of Allah ﷻ. The greatest *jihad* is the one that makes us better people inside. It means following the teachings of Islam and trying to make oneself a true believer. It is also *jihad* to share our wealth and our time with others who are in need. But *jihad* can also mean struggling with both words and weapons against those who try to destroy Islam as well as those who try to harm or kill innocent people.

The strong faith of the Muslims pleased Allah ﷻ. He knew they were few in number. Allah ﷻ knew that the Muslims had very few weapons and almost no armor. He sent angels to help the Muslims fight. In the end they won a great victory.

Many of the leaders of the *Kuffar* fell in the battle, and several of their warriors were taken prisoner. They felt ashamed of their loss. "We want revenge!" their chiefs said. "We will fight again. And next time we will not lose!"

Rules of War

Shortly before his passing away, Rasulullah ﷺ appointed the youthful 'Usama ibn Zaid ﷜ to lead a military expedition against the Romans. But the Prophet ﷺ did not live long enough to see it and it was up to Khalifah Abu Bakr ﷛ to make sure 'Usama ﷜ and his men were sent out. But before he left, Abu Bakr ﷛ gave 'Usama ﷜ very important guidance on how he and his men should conduct themselves. This later became the standard rules of how Muslims should conduct themselves in times of war:

"Do not deceive anyone, even your enemy. Do not hoard the treasures you capture in battle. Do not mutilate anyone, even the dead. Do not slay old people, children or women. Do not set fire to the date-palms. Do not cut down the fruit trees. Do not slaughter goats, or cows, or camels except if needed to feed yourselves. Also you will come across Christian people who have given up the world and are living in monasteries. Leave them alone and cause them no harm."

Prophet Muhammad ﷺ and his *Sahabah* ﷜ thanked Allah ﷻ for their victory. They knew that they had won only because of Allah's help.

Prophet Muhammad ﷺ told the Muslims to treat all the prisoners kindly. Some were freed after paying a ransom and were allowed to return to Makkah. Others earned their freedom by teaching Muslims how to read and write.

In those days it was common for victorious armies to execute enemies captured in battle. But Allah ﷻ gave the Muslims rules for both war and peace. Muslims cannot do whatever they please, but they have to follow what Allah ﷻ and His Messenger decide. Prophet Muhammad ﷺ told the Muslims to treat their enemies fairly. A Muslim can never mistreat those captured in war. Because they were treated in a good way, many of the enemy prisoners realized that Prophet Muhammad ﷺ was truly Allah's Messenger and that Islam was the true religion. They became Muslims and stayed in Madinah.

WE HAVE LEARNED

- In Madinah Allah ﷻ ordered the Muslims to defend themselves.
- At the Battle of Badr, the small army of Muslims defeated the large army of the *Kuffar*.
- The Muslims treated their prisoners kindly, and some of them accepted Islam and stayed in Madinah.

WORDS TO KNOW

Abuse, Humiliated, *Jihad*, Persecute, Prisoner, Ransom

QUR'AN CONNECTION

Allah ﷻ speaks about *jihad* in the Qur'an:

وَٱلَّذِينَ جَٰهَدُواْ فِينَا لَنَهْدِيَنَّهُمْ سُبُلَنَا ۚ وَإِنَّ ٱللَّهَ لَمَعَ ٱلْمُحْسِنِينَ ۝

"And those who strive for Us, We will surely guide them to Our paths. And, indeed, Allah is with those who do good."

(al-Ankabut 29:69)

Lesson 7

The Battle of Uhud
(The 3rd year of the *Hijrah*)

Looking Ahead

After their defeat at the Battle of Badr, the *Kuffar* wanted revenge. Read how the next battle nearly became a defeat for the Muslims.

The *Kuffar* of Makkah were furious after their defeat at the Battle of Badr. They began planning for another attack.

Almost one year after Badr, an army of nearly three thousand *Kuffar* came to attack Madinah. The Muslim army numbered only 1,000. There were also 300 *Munafiqun* in the Muslim army. The *Munafiqun* left the army before the battle started and tried to get other Muslims to do the same. They hoped that their leaving would make the Muslims lose heart. They also expected that the large size of the enemy force would frighten the Muslims into giving up.

But the Muslims' faith and commitment were firm. "We will never leave our Prophet," they said. "If we live, we will live as Muslims. If we have to die, we want to die fighting for the Truth."

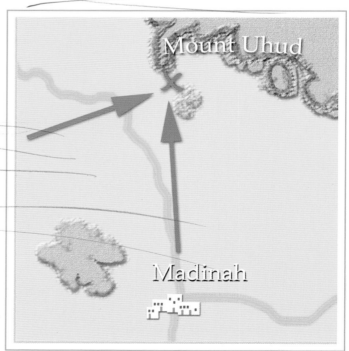

The Muslims marched north to meet the Makkan *Kuffar* near Mount Uhud.

The two armies soon faced each other near a mountain called Uhud. This mountain was about three miles north of Madinah. There were 3,000 *Kuffar* against 700 Muslims. The battle started quickly. At first the *Kuffar* were losing the battle and many of them started to run away. The Muslims were overjoyed thinking they had

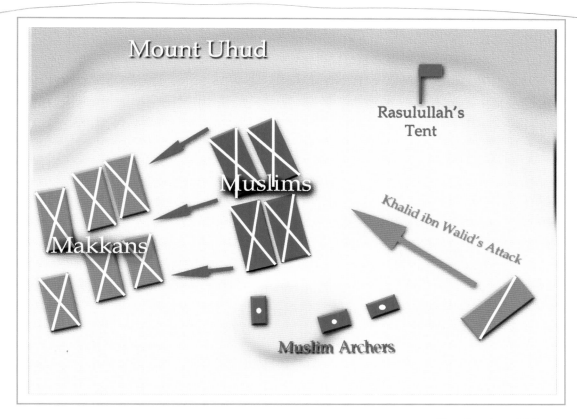

The Battle of Uhud

won the day. They ran forward to chase the *Kuffar* and gather up the weapons and supplies left behind.

The *Kuffar*, however, sent some of their horsemen through a mountain pass to hit the Muslims from behind. Before the battle started, Rasulullah ﷺ had told some archers to guard a hill so that the back of the Muslim army would be protected. They were told not to leave that hill no matter what. But when the archers guarding the pass saw the enemy running away, most of them left their post. They wanted to take their share of the booty. Only a few archers remained to guard the pass despite Rasulullah's order.

Seeing that the hill was unguarded, the horsemen of the *Kuffar* rode around the unprotected hill and attacked the Muslims from behind. A fierce fight followed. Many of the believers were killed, and many others were wounded. Rasulullah ﷺ himself was wounded and the *Kuffar* began to shout that they had killed him. When the Muslims heard this, they were shocked and started losing their courage.

Even though Rasulullah ﷺ was wounded, he was safe. Those *Sahabah* near to him protected him at every side. They helped him to go up to the mountain to his tent where it was safe. When the Muslims learned that Rasulullah ﷺ was alive and well they were very relieved.

Both sides were exhausted by the fighting. Many dead lay on both sides. Although they did not completely defeat the Muslims, the *Kuffar* believed they had gotten revenge for their defeat at the Battle of Badr.

The Muslims were saddened because many of their brothers had been killed in the battle. Rasulullah's own uncle, Hamza ﷺ, was killed and his body mutilated. The Muslims also remembered that some had followed the *Munafiqun* and stayed home and still others had disobeyed Rasulullah's order to guard the hill. They understood that the loss of so many lives was the result of not obeying Rasulullah's orders.

Then Allah ﷻ sent *wahi* concerning the Battle of Uhud. He told the Muslims to be patient and put their trust in Him. Their faith would be tested in many ways, but Allah ﷻ promised to give the believers victory if they remained faithful.

After the Battle of Uhud, the *Kuffar* and their friends became very bold. Some of these people even went so far as to deceive the Muslims. They would invite Muslims to come and teach them Islam, but when they came they would be slain. It was a very difficult time for the Believers. But they remained patient, obeyed their Prophet ﷺ, and prayed to Allah ﷻ for help.

WE HAVE LEARNED

- A large army of *Kuffar* fought against the Muslims at Uhud.
- At first the Muslims were winning, but after they disobeyed Rasulullah ﷺ, the *Kuffar* attacked them through the pass.
- The Muslims suffered great losses. Allah ﷻ told them to be patient.

WORDS TO KNOW

Bold, Fierce, Mutilate, Tragedy, Uhud

QUR'AN CONNECTION

Allah ﷻ speaks about the losses of the Battle of Uhud in the Qur'an:

يَـٰٓأَيُّهَا ٱلَّذِينَ ءَامَنُوا۟ ٱسْتَعِينُوا۟ بِٱلصَّبْرِ وَٱلصَّلَوٰةِ
إِنَّ ٱللَّهَ مَعَ ٱلصَّـٰبِرِينَ ۝ وَلَا تَقُولُوا۟ لِمَن يُقْتَلُ فِى سَبِيلِ ٱللَّهِ
أَمْوَٰتٌۢ بَلْ أَحْيَآءٌ وَلَـٰكِن لَّا تَشْعُرُونَ ۝

*"O you who believe! Seek help through patience and Salat.
Certainly Allah is with those who are patient. And say not of those who are
killed in the Way of Allah, 'They are dead.' No, they are living, though you
do not see it."*

(al-Baqarah 2:153-154)

Lesson 8

The Battle of the Ditch
(The 5th year of the *Hijrah*)

Looking Ahead

The *Kuffar* and their allies made one last try to destroy the Muslim *Ummah*. Let's read why this battle was called the "Battle of the Ditch."

The *Kuffar* were pleased that they inflicted heavy losses on the Muslims at the Battle of Uhud. Yet they were not completely satisfied with their success. The battle had not decided anything, since the Muslims were still there. In fact, the Muslims' strength only seemed to increase.

After nearly two years of preparation, the *Kuffar* and their allies decided to make one more attack on Madinah. They gathered a huge army of nearly 24,000 men. They wanted it to be a battle that would put an end to Islam once and for all.

The Muslims could not hope to gather enough men to face such an army. How could they fight and defend their homes? One of the *Sahabah* had an idea. His name was Salman al-Farsi, and he was originally from Persia. He said, "In our country, when we are weak, we dig a deep ditch around our towns to slow the enemy's attack."

Rasulullah liked Salman's idea, and the Muslims began to dig a deep ditch around Madinah. It was a difficult task, because the land was rocky and hard and the enemy would soon be there. Rasulullah and his *Sahabah* worked day and night digging the ditch. It was finally completed right before the huge army of the *Kuffar* arrived.

When they reached Madinah, the *Kuffar* and their allies found the ditch and did not know what to do. They had never faced a ditch in battle before. Since crossing it would be nearly impossible, they set up their tents on the other side. Each day a few of their brave warriors tried to cross the ditch, but the Muslims would beat them back.

Many days and nights passed. The food supply for Madinah was running low. The Muslims were tired and hungry, but they did not think of surrendering. During the battle the Muslims made all their *salat*.

After nearly a month had passed, Rasulullah ﷺ prayed to Allah ﷻ for this hardship to end. Allah ﷻ knew how courageous the believers were and He promised a victory if they kept their faith. No one could imagine that such a small number of Muslims could win over such an enormous army.

The very next night, Allah ﷻ sent a powerful wind which tore apart the tents of the *Kuffar*. Their horses and camels became frightened and ran away. Thinking that the Muslims were attacking, the *Kuffar* even fought among themselves because they couldn't see through all the blowing sand. Finally, their whole army fled away in confusion.

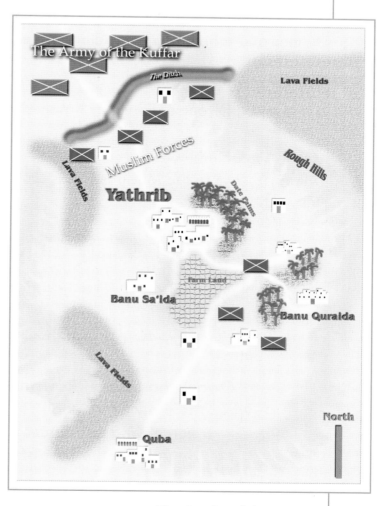

The Battle of the Ditch

The Muslims were given an unexpected victory. Allah ﷻ rewarded their faith and patience. How great was His help! How thankful Rasulullah ﷺ and the Muslims were for His kindness!

WE HAVE LEARNED

- The *Kuffar* and their supporters attacked the Muslims with a huge army.
- The Muslims dug a ditch around Madinah to protect themselves and the city.
- After one month of siege, Allah ﷻ sent a wind to disperse the *Kuffar*.

WORDS TO KNOW

Confusion, Disperse, Fervently, Impossible, Persia, Pitch

QUR'AN CONNECTION

Allah ﷻ says to the Muslims in the Qur'an about His favor:

$$\text{يَٰٓأَيُّهَا ٱلَّذِينَ ءَامَنُوا۟ ٱذْكُرُوا۟ نِعْمَةَ ٱللَّهِ}$$
$$\text{عَلَيْكُمْ إِذْ جَآءَتْكُمْ جُنُودٌ فَأَرْسَلْنَا عَلَيْهِمْ رِيحًا وَجُنُودًا لَّمْ}$$
$$\text{تَرَوْهَا ۚ وَكَانَ ٱللَّهُ بِمَا تَعْمَلُونَ بَصِيرًا ﴿٩﴾}$$

"O you who believe! Remember the favor of Allah to you,
when the army came upon you. Then We sent against them
a fierce wind and forces which you could not see.
Allah is the Seer of what ever you do."

(al-Ahzab 33:9)

Lesson 9

Prophet Muhammad Leads a Community

Looking Ahead

Madinah quickly turned into a community. We will read here how Rasulullah ﷺ managed the affairs of the community and established an effective government.

When Rasulullah ﷺ arrived in Madinah he was asked to become the city's leader. As a leader he earned the trust of his people and helped them in solving their problems. Not only did he guide them on the Path of Islam, but he also settled disputes and arguments as well. Sometimes he was forced to lead his men out to fight those who wanted to attack Madinah.

Before Islam came to them, the two main tribes of Madinah, the 'Aws and the Khazraj, constantly fought each other. As their members embraced Islam, Rasulullah ﷺ told them to put behind their quarrels and become brothers and sisters. In this way the Prophet ﷺ brought peace to Madinah. The *Muwakhat* also brought the Muslims closer to one another. Slowly people stopped looking at themselves as belonging to different tribes and, instead, now saw themselves as Muslims.

As a leader, Rasulullah ﷺ showed great concern for anyone who was hurting or suffering. The Qur'an describes his concern in the following verse:

$$لَقَدْ جَآءَكُمْ رَسُولٌ مِّنْ أَنفُسِكُمْ عَزِيزٌ عَلَيْهِ$$
$$مَا عَنِتُّمْ حَرِيصٌ عَلَيْكُم بِالْمُؤْمِنِينَ رَءُوفٌ رَّحِيمٌ ۝$$

"There has come to you a Messenger from among yourselves; it grieves him to see you suffering; he is worried about you, full of concern for you, for the believers full of pity, compassion."

(al-Tawbah, 9:128)

When one of *Sahabah* passed away, Rasulullah ﷺ asked those present at the funeral whether that person had left behind any unpaid debt. If he did, Rasulullah ﷺ would say, "I am this person's guardian. I will pay off what is left of his or her debt."

Rasulullah ﷺ had always tried hard to live in peace with those tribes in Madinah that followed Judaism. He thought that they would be pleased to live together with the Muslims since they both believed in One God. But their chiefs broke their agreement with Rasulullah ﷺ and aided the *Kuffar* in their struggle against the Muslims. The Muslims were forced to fight in order to protect themselves. One by one, the Jewish tribes were defeated and moved out of Madinah.

The people of Khaibar lived in great fortresses much like these.

Two of the Jewish tribes left Madinah and moved north to an oasis called Khaibar. They built strong fortresses there. These two tribes still wanted to fight the Muslims, but in a battle at Khaibar they were defeated. After the battle they asked to live in peace with the Muslims. Rasulullah ﷺ agreed to allow them to live peacefully in Khaibar. He treated the Jewish people with fairness.

Despite having many enemies, the Prophet Muhammad ﷺ was always quick to forgive those who fought against him. For instance, he knew that Ibn Ubai and the *Munafiqun* secretly plotted against the Muslims, but he did not harm them. He let them continue to live in Madinah, and they enjoyed the same rights as other Muslims.

In doing this, Rasulullah ﷺ showed us that we must judge people according to their actions; we cannot pry into whether people are being truthful in their beliefs or not.

Prophet Muhammad ﷺ was a leader who had great power. His *Sahabah* would have given everything to him: money, food and property. In spite of this

Rasulullah ﷺ lived a very plain and simple life. He slept every night on a straw mat with only a sheepskin as a blanket. Sometimes he and his family would go to sleep without food because he gave it all away to the needy. Although many of his *Sahabah* were very rich, Rasulullah ﷺ wanted to live like the poorest of his people.

In all of his words and actions Rasulullah ﷺ was a living example of the teachings of Qur'an. His perfect life of goodness helped people to fix their hearts firmly on Allah ﷻ. We are fortunate that many of his sayings and actions have been recorded by his *Sahabah* in collections called *Hadith* to serve guides for us.

WE HAVE LEARNED

- The fighting tribes of 'Aws and Khazraj gave up their disputes and became brothers after accepting Islam and listening to Rasulullah ﷺ.
- The Jewish tribes of Madinah moved away to a place called Khaibar.
- Rasulullah ﷺ lived a very simple life teaching people the message of the Qur'an.

WORDS TO KNOW

Dispute, Debt, Fortress, Guide, Protect

HADITH CONNECTION

Rasulullah ﷺ said about the community of believers:

HONOR AND REVENGE

Unlike most other people living in the 7th century CE, the Arabs did not have a central government that ruled over them. Every tribe was like a country unto itself. Since they had no state, there were few laws that could be enforced. The rich and powerful could basically do as they pleased and those who had neither money nor strength suffered immensely at their hands. Slaves, the poor and those without attachment to a strong tribe were easy to abuse. Females were seen as property, although some became quite influential. If a man had no sons and only daughters, he could kill his young daughters out of embarrassment.

Honor was also source of pride among the Arabs. If an individual's honor was insulted in any way, revenge would be required at all cost. This very often led to killing and it soon involved entire tribes. If one member of a tribe was murdered (justly or unjustly) the entire tribe was obliged to avenge the death of its kinsman. Full-scale wars would break out between tribes over a killing that resulted, say, from the theft of a sheep. Feuds between tribes could often last for generations, as with the 'Aws and the Khazraj.

"The example of the believers in their love and mercy for each other is like the example of a body; if one part of the body hurts, the entire body will feel it."

(*Muslim, Musnad Ahmad*)

Lesson 10

The Treaty of Hudaibiyah
(The 6th year of the *Hijrah*)

Looking Ahead

The *Kuffar* became afraid of continuing their fight against the Muslims. It now looked like they wanted peace.

After the victory at the Battle of the Ditch, the Muslims felt safe from anymore attacks. The *Kuffar* had been defeated. The Jewish tribes of Madinah had moved away. Many of the *Munafiqun* came to the Believers and said, "We honestly believe in Allah and His Prophet. We wish to become true Muslims." At this time Rasulullah ﷺ decided to go to Makkah to perform *Umrah*.

As we have learned in earlier readings, the Ka`bah was built hundreds of years earlier by Prophet Ibrahim and his son Isma`il ﷺ. Over the years the Arabs had turned the Ka'bah into a house for idols.

Still, the Ka`bah was sacred to all the Arabs, and everyone tried their best to visit it. But the *Kuffar* disliked the Muslims so much that up to now they had not given them the freedom to visit the Ka`bah.

Rasulullah's decision to perform *Umrah* pleased the Muslims. The *Muhajirun* were especially happy. They wanted to go back to see the city which they loved in addition to visiting the Ka`bah.

The Muslims set up their tents in the Valley of Hudaibiyah.

As the Muslims prepared to go for *Umrah,* they took many animals with them to sacrifice. The Muslims were excited to think that they were finally going to Makkah to worship Allah ﷻ. After many days of preparation they set out from Madinah.

After nearly two weeks of travel the Muslims came to a place called Hudaibiyah. They came in peace, but the chiefs of the *Kuffar* would not allow them to enter the city. Rasulullah ﷺ and his *Sahabah* did not want anymore fighting or killing. So they waited outside Makkah, trying to agree with the chiefs to get permission to perform *Umrah.*

Some Muslims were ready to fight for the right to make *Umrah.* But Rasulullah ﷺ told them, "We have come here to perform a peaceful *Umrah.* There will be no fighting." He sent his son-in-law 'Uthman ﷺ to tell this to the chiefs, but they did not agree. Instead they said they would be prepared to fight if need be. Rasulullah ﷺ waited patiently.

At last, the chiefs sent one of their leaders to the Prophet ﷺ. "This year we will not allow you to perform *Umrah,*" the envoy said, "But next year we will let you come back. Then you can make it." He also told Rasulullah ﷺ that they were now ready to sign a peace treaty with the Muslims.

The Muslims were very eager to perform *Umrah.* Since they were Arabs, they felt they had a right to visit the Ka`bah. They were not ready to accept this offer from the *Kuffar.* But Rasulullah ﷺ knew how important it was for the Muslims to have peace so he agreed to the proposal.

The *Kuffar* and the Muslims made an agreement. This agreement is called the Treaty of Hudaibiyah. The terms of the agreement did not seem fair to many Muslims, and some *Sahabah* were not happy about it. But given that Rasulullah ﷺ entered into the agreement, all the Muslims accepted it.

By accepting this agreement, Rasulullah ﷺ let everyone see that he and the Muslims wanted compromise and not conflict. Islam is a way of peace. At times war cannot be avoided, but peace is better for everyone than fighting.

The Muslims returned to Madinah unhappy about not being allowed to perform *Umrah*. Some thought of this as a sort of defeat. Then Allah ﷻ sent *wahi*, and in this *wahi* the peace treaty was called "a clear victory."

The Treaty of Hudaibiyah contained many terms. One of these was that if a Makkan accepted Islam and went to Madinah, he would have to be sent back. Right after the treaty was signed, a Makkan named Abu Jandal traveled to Madinah to see Rasulullah ﷺ. He recently embraced Islam and the *Kuffar* treated him very badly. But the agreement required Rasulullah ﷺ to send him back.

The Treaty of Hudaibiyah

"These are the terms of the truce between Muhammad, the son of `Abdullah and Suhail, the son of `Amr.

Both groups have agreed not to fight for ten years.
During this time, each group shall be safe, and neither shall attack the other; no secret plans will be made, but uprightness and honor will exist between them.

The Muslims will return to Madinah this year without performing *Umrah*. Next year they can make it. They can stay in Makkah for three days, with no weapons except those for safe traveling, with swords remaining in their sheaths.

If a Makkan comes to Muhammad without the permission of his guardian, Muhammad must return him, but if one of Muhammad's people comes to Makkah, he will not be returned.

Whoever wishes to enter into an alliance with Muhammad can do so, and whoever wishes to enter into alliance with the Quraish can do so."

"Abu Jandal," said Rasulullah ﷺ, "I cannot break my word, even with those who are against me. It breaks my heart, but you have to go back. We Muslims cannot break our promises. Allah ﷻ will find a way out for you." And so Abu Jandal went back to Makkah where the *Kuffar* punished him.

The Muslims looked forward to the following year in order to perform *Umrah*. But during the year of waiting much happened in Madinah.

WE HAVE LEARNED
- Prophet Muhammad ﷺ and the Muslims went to Makkah to perform *Umrah*, but the *Kuffar* did not allow them to enter the city.
- The Muslims and the *Kuffar* signed a peace agreement.
- Some *Sahabah* were not happy about the agreement, but Allah ﷻ called it "a clear victory."

WORDS TO KNOW
Bloodshed, Envoy, Perform, Sacred, *Umrah*

QUR'AN CONNECTION
Allah ﷻ speaks in the Qur'an about respecting agreements:

$$\text{فَأَتِمُّوٓاْ إِلَيۡهِمۡ عَهۡدَهُمۡ إِلَىٰ مُدَّتِهِمۡ ۚ إِنَّ ٱللَّهَ يُحِبُّ ٱلۡمُتَّقِينَ}$$

"Then fulfill the agreements you have made with them until the end of their time. Certainly Allah loves those who are righteous ."

(al-Tawbah 9:4)

The Clear Victory
(The 6th Year of the *Hijrah*)

Looking Ahead

Despite its drawbacks, the Treaty of Hudaibiyah was a great blessing in disguise for the Muslims.

The Treaty of Hudaibiyah proved to be a great blessing for the Muslims. Before it was signed, no non-believer had been able to visit Madinah because of the conflict between the *Kuffar* and the Muslims. Now that there was peace, many non-Muslims came to Madinah. They met Rasulullah ﷺ, heard the Qur'an and visited with the Muslims. Many of these people accepted Islam.

Likewise, the Muslims were now able to meet many tribes throughout Arabia without worry of being attacked. They spoke to the people about the teachings of Islam. The tribes saw that the Muslims behaved differently than other people. They saw that the Muslims feared the One God, Allah ﷻ, and prayed and fasted. They told the truth, they kept their promises, and they helped others. They did not drink alchohol or gamble or use rude language. People were so impressed by the good behavior of the Muslims that they decided to accept Islam themselves.

Islam is the religion for all people. In fact, Rasulullah ﷺ was sent as "A Mercy for all Mankind," not just for the Arabs. It was at this time that Allah ﷻ told Rasulullah ﷺ to invite the people of the world to Islam.

To do this Rasulullah ﷺ wrote letters to the leaders of the countries that surrounded Arabia, including the ruler of the Roman Empire, the Shah of Persia, the King of Ethiopia and the governor of Egypt. He asked these important rulers to believe in One God and he warned them that the Day of Judgment was sure to come, a day when Allah ﷻ would judge our actions.

THINK ABOUT IT
What are some of the things you can do to show others that Islam is a religion of peace and caring?

As we read in *Mercy to Mankind: Life in Makkah*, the King of Ethiopia believed in Rasulullah ﷺ in his heart. But he could not openly express his belief. The powerful Emperor of the Rome, as well as the governor of Egypt, decided to keep their own religion. Nevertheless they gave respect to Rasulullah ﷺ and sent him gifts.

However the ruler of the Persian Empire, the *Shah*, was not as friendly. He spoke rudely about Rasulullah ﷺ and warned that if he was captured by the Persians

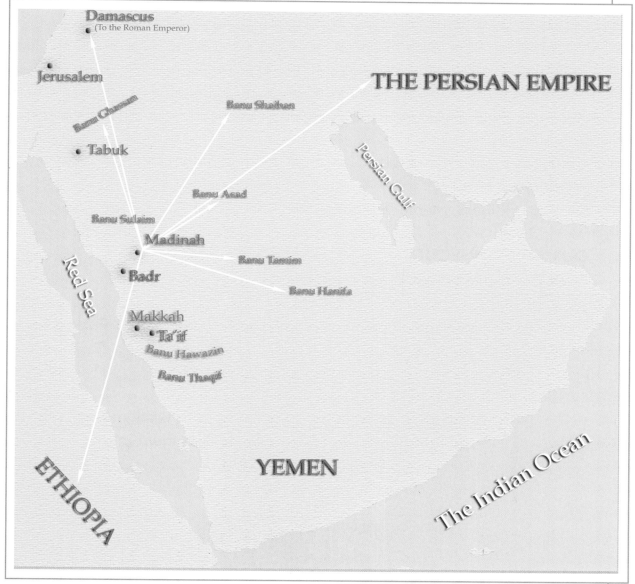

The Prophet sent out messengers to the rulers of the world.

he would be executed. Such words did not bother Rasulullah ﷺ. He knew that Allah ﷻ is the Best Protector.

More and more people in the world started knowing about Allah's Final Message. The *Kuffar* were not happy seeing Islam spreading throughout Arabia. They regretted making peace with the Muslims. Now they realized how the treaty had helped the Muslims. Some of their chiefs now made up their minds to break it.

WE HAVE LEARNED
- The Treaty of Hudaibiyah made it possible for many more people to learn about Prophet Muhammad ﷺ and the Muslims.
- Many people who did not believe before now accepted Islam.
- The Prophet ﷺ sent letters to kings and rulers of the world to invite them to Islam.

WORDS TO KNOW
Blessing, Ethiopia, Mercy, *Shah*, Spread

QUR'AN CONNECTION
Allah ﷻ speaks about calling people to Islam,

$$ٱدْعُ إِلَىٰ سَبِيلِ رَبِّكَ بِٱلْحِكْمَةِ وَٱلْمَوْعِظَةِ ٱلْحَسَنَةِ ۖ وَجَٰدِلْهُم بِٱلَّتِى هِىَ أَحْسَنُ$$

"Invite people to the way of your Lord with wisdom and beautiful teachings. And discuss with them in ways which are best."

(an-Nahl 16:125)

Lesson 12

The March to Makkah
(The 7th year of the *Hijrah*)

Looking Ahead

With the treaty broken, Rasulullah ﷺ decided to march to Makkah and clear the Ka`bah of idols once and for all.

Soon the *Kuffar* understood that they made a big mistake in offering peace to the Muslims, for now Islam was spreading everywhere. To stop this they decided to break the treaty. They had some of their allies ambush a group of Muslims in the desert. When this happened, the Treaty of Hudaibiyah was called off. After it was broken, the Muslims took action to punish the *Kuffar*.

Allah ﷻ told Rasulullah ﷺ to assemble a large army and go to Makkah. It was time for the Ka`bah, the ancient House of Allah, to be cleaned of idol worship. Seven years earlier, Rasulullah ﷺ and the *Muhajirun* had been forced to leave their homes in Makkah. Now they were ready to enter their home city.

Rasulullah ﷺ led an army of almost 10,000 out of Madinah. As they marched through the desert many tribes joined them along the way. The Muslim army stopped just outside Makkah. When the *Kuffar* saw this force they were terrified. Abu Sufian, their leader, came out to see the Muslim army. He was captured and brought before Rasulullah ﷺ.

Abu Sufian thought for sure that he would be executed. "We have not come to kill," Rasulullah ﷺ

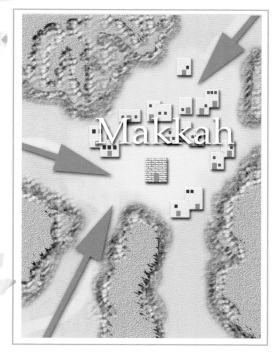

The Muslims advanced on Makkah from all sides

told Abu Sufian. "We have come to cleanse the Ka`bah of all idols and make it the House of Allah once again. We do not want revenge. We will not fight those who do not fight us."

Abu Sufian could hardly believe Rasulullah's words. He had not expected the Prophet ﷺ to be so kind after all the *Kuffar* had done to the Muslims. But he knew that Rasulullah ﷺ always told the truth and always kept his word.

Allah ﷻ opened Abu Sufian's heart to Islam and he became Muslim right there. Rasulullah ﷺ then asked Abu Sufian to go back to Makkah and give its people his message of peace. "Tell the people of Makkah that all those who do not fight us will be safe. If they stay in the residence of Abu Sufian or in their own homes or even in the Ka`bah, no harm will come to them."

WE HAVE LEARNED
- Rasulullah ﷺ decided to cleanse the Ka'bah of its idols.
- Abu Sufian, the leader of the *Kuffar*, accepted Islam.
- Prophet Muhammad ﷺ promised safety for all the people of Makkah if they did not fight against the Muslims.

WORDS TO KNOW
Guidance, Cleanse, Revenge

QUR'AN CONNECTION
Allah ﷻ tells us about His Promise in the Qur'an:

$$هُوَ ٱلَّذِىٓ أَرْسَلَ رَسُولَهُۥ بِٱلْهُدَىٰ وَدِينِ ٱلْحَقِّ لِيُظْهِرَهُۥ عَلَى ٱلدِّينِ كُلِّهِۦ وَلَوْ كَرِهَ ٱلْمُشْرِكُونَ ﴿٩﴾$$

"It is He who sent His Messenger with guidance and the true way of life, that He may proclaim it over all other ways of life, even though the polytheists may not like it."

(*as-Saff* 61:9)

Lesson 13

The Ka`bah is Cleansed

Looking Ahead

The Ka`bah was finally restored to the worship of One God. This is the purpose for which it was built by Prophet Ibrahim ﷺ centuries before.

The people of Makkah saw the strength of Muslim army. But they also saw the kindness and mercy of Rasulullah ﷺ. "Only a true man of God could be so kind," they thought. Many of them were now ready to believe in him.

The Muslim army entered Makkah. *"Allahu Akbar*! Allah is Greatest!" they called out, "Allah has given us victory!" They had come to bring the religion of Allah ﷻ, not to fight or take revenge. Rasulullah ﷺ entered the Ka`bah with his cousin 'Ali ﷺ and removed all the idols. The Ka`bah was once again the House of Allah just as Prophet Ibrahim ﷺ had intended.

THE STORY OF THE KA`BAH

The Ka`bah was originally built by Prophet Adam ﷺ thousands of years ago after the Angel Jibril ﷺ brought the Black Stone down from heaven. By the time of Prophet Ibrahim ﷺ, the original building no longer existed and it had to be rebuilt. Many years after Prophet Ibrahim and his son, Prophet Isma`il ﷺ, rebuilt the Ka`bah, the Arabs turned it from place for worshiping One God to a house of idols. Nevertheless, for many hundreds of years the Ka`bah was still a holy place for the tribes of Arabia and every year people would come there to pray to their gods and goddesses.

In the year 570 CE, the mighty king of Yemen, Abraha, decided to send an army to tear down the Ka`bah. But his plan was stopped by a miracle and the sacred building was saved. Several years later, when the Prophet Muhammad ﷺ was a young man, the Ka`bah was destroyed by a flood. All of the tribes of Makkah came together to rebuild it. They all argued over who would have the honor of placing the Black Stone back into its place. To avoid a fight they decided that the first person to step through the gate of the wall surrounding the Ka`bah should be the one to decide who was to put the stone in its place. Just then the young Muhammad ﷺ passed through the gate. In his wisdom Muhammad ﷺ told the men to bring a big sheet and to put the stone on it. All the chiefs of the tribes would lift the sheet together and he would then put the stone in its place. In this way the Prophet ﷺ allowed all the tribes to have the honor of this great act.

The Ka`bah has been rebuilt and the *masjid* around it renovated several times after the Prophet's passing away. The most recent renovations to the al-*Haram ash-Sharif* (the Ka`bah and the area around it) were done in the 1970's. That's when the huge beautiful *masjid* that we now see around it was built.

Rasulullah ﷺ then made a speech:

"Allah is One.
He promised to help us, and indeed He has helped us
and has given us victory.
O People of Quraish! You should not be proud of your tribe.
All of us are the children of Adam,
and Adam was made from dust.
We should be kind to one another
and should not take revenge on each other.
Allah loves those who are good and kind."

The *Kuffar* listened to Rasulullah ﷺ with attention. "He is so noble and upright!" they said, "Perhaps we were wrong to stand against him." Then they accepted Islam and became a part of the growing *Ummah* of Muhammad ﷺ.

Many people thought that Rasulullah ﷺ and the *Muhajirun* would stay in Makkah. They expected them to take back their homes and property from those who seized them years earlier. But Rasulullah ﷺ told the *Muhajirun*, "Allah has given us Islam. That is enough for us. Do not take anything back from the Makkans. They are your brothers and sisters from this day forward."

"The Makkans have accepted Islam," said the *Muhajirun*. "They are part of our *Ummah* now. We forgive them for what they did to us in the past. We do not want to take anything from them. Allah and His Prophet are enough for us."

The *Ansar* were sad, fearing that the Prophet ﷺ would leave Madinah and move back to Makkah. But Rasulullah ﷺ spoke to them. "I will not leave you," he said, "and I will live the rest of my life with you in Madinah." The *Ansar* were so happy with these words that some of them cried.

The *Muhajirun* said, "We shall never leave our Prophet. We left Makkah for his sake. Madinah is the city of our Prophet and it is our city. We shall stay in Madinah too."

WE HAVE LEARNED

- The Prophet ﷺ made the Ka`bah a place for the worship of Allah ﷻ alone once again.
- In his speech Rasulullah ﷺ said, "No one should be proud of his or her tribe. All of us are children of Adam. We should be kind to each other."
- The *Muhajirun* did not take anything back from the Makkans.

WORDS TO KNOW

Allahu Akbar, Generous, Expected

QUR'AN CONNECTION

Allah ﷻ speaks about forgivness of past wrongs,

$$ وَمَن يَعْمَلْ سُوٓءًا أَوْ يَظْلِمْ نَفْسَهُۥ ثُمَّ يَسْتَغْفِرِ ٱللَّهَ يَجِدِ ٱللَّهَ غَفُورًا رَّحِيمًا ۝ $$

"And whoever does evil or acts unjustly to his soul, and then asks forgiveness of Allah, he shall find Allah Forgiving, Merciful."

(*an-Nisa* 4:110)

Lesson 14

The Battle of Hunain
(The 8th year of the *Hijrah*)

Looking Ahead

There were warrior tribes living in the rugged hills around Ta'if who worshipped idols. They planned to attack the Muslims in Makkah.

Although most of the people of Makkah had now accepted Islam, there were still tribes that clung to their idols. When the news of what had happened in Makkah reached tribes living in the town of Ta'if they became furious. They began thinking about having one final battle with the Muslims.

While he was still in Makkah, Rasulullah ﷺ heard that the tribes of Ta'if were getting ready to attack. He decided to strike before they could reach Makkah. This time, the Muslim army was very large. The *Ansar*, the *Muhajirun*, and the new Muslims of Makkah joined together under the flag of Rasulullah ﷺ. Some Muslims thought, "Today our number is great and our army is strong. No one can beat us." They had become proud of their strength and thought that they would easily defeat their enemies. But Allah ﷻ wanted to teach them a different lesson.

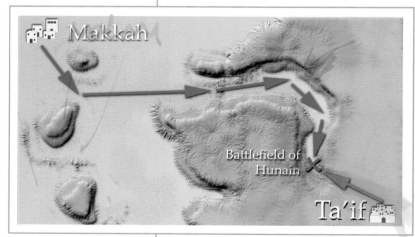

The Muslim march from Makkah.

The Muslim army faced the tribes in a valley called Hunain, which was to the east of Makkah. The people of Ta'if had skilled archers, and from the mountainsides they showered the Muslim army with arrows killing many. The Muslims were surprised and started to flee. Allah showed them that it is not numbers but only He who gives victory. As most of the Muslim army started to run away, Rasulullah ﷺ stood firm with a few of his *Sahabah*. He was not afraid, even though arrows were falling all around him. When he saw the Muslims running away he called out, "Come back, O Believers! I am indeed the Prophet of Allah! There is no reason to fear!"

When the Muslims heard Rasulullah's call it gave them courage. They realized their mistake in running away. They asked Allah ﷻ to forgive their weakness and help them win the battle. They returned to the side of Rasulullah ﷺ with renewed faith.

A fierce battle followed, and the Ta'ifans were completely defeated. The Muslims captured many of their enemy, and obtained a large amount of supplies. Rasulullah ﷺ ordered the prisoners to be treated kindly. Later he even ordered that their property be returned to them. Eventually the tribes of Ta'if embraced Islam.

WE HAVE LEARNED

- Many Muslims were confident of their large numbers and great strength.
- Victory and defeat come from Allah ﷻ alone.
- The Muslims were kind and generous to their enemies.

WORDS TO KNOW

Archers, Fierce, Hunain, Ta'if

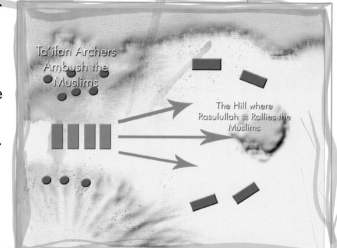

The Battle of Hunain. The Muslim forces are in green. The Ta'ifans in red.

QUR'AN CONNECTION

Allah ﷻ says about His help,

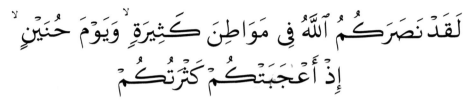

لَقَدْ نَصَرَكُمُ ٱللَّهُ فِى مَوَاطِنَ كَثِيرَةٍ وَيَوْمَ حُنَيْنٍ إِذْ أَعْجَبَتْكُمْ كَثْرَتُكُمْ

"Indeed, Allah helped you on many battlefields and on the day of Hunain when you boasted about your great numbers..."

(at-Tawbah 9:25)

Lesson 15 — Meeting the Roman Empire (1)

Looking Ahead

Beyond the deserts of northern Arabia were two great civilizations. For the first time the Muslims came into contact with the armies of the Roman Empire.

After he left Makkah and returned to Madinah, the Prophet Muhammad ﷺ spent all his time teaching Islam. Every day more tribes came and accepted Islam. Muslims traveled all over the Arabian Peninsula to invite people to Islam. Islam was spreading quickly throughout the land.

When the rulers of the Roman Empire far to the north of Madinah heard that the Arabs were embracing a new religion, they became concerned.

Most of the people living in the Roman Empire followed the religion of Christianity. It was the main religion in parts of Asia, Europe and Africa at the time Prophet Muhammad ﷺ was born. Many of the Arab people living in Yemen and Syria were also Christians. However in central Arabia, where Makkah was, there were only a few Christians. In this region, most people worshipped idols and prayed to many gods.

During one of his early trips to Syria with his uncle Abu Talib, the young Muhammad ﷺ met a Christian monk called Bahira.

Two great empires dominated the Middle East during the time of Rasulullah ﷺ.

He was a pious man and he recognized that there was something very special about this boy named Muhammad. Bahira told Abu Talib that his nephew would one day become a great prophet and that the people of Makkah would fight against him.

Many years later when Muhammad ﷺ received the first Revelation of the Qur'an in the Cave of Hira, he was frightened. He went to his wife Khadijah ﷺ and she comforted him. She then took him to her cousin Waraqa ibn Nawfil, who was a Christian. Waraqa was a deeply religious man and he was very learned in his religion. He told Khadijah ﷺ that Prophet Muhammad ﷺ was visited by the same angel who came to all the prophets before. But Waraqa was very old and he wished that he could live long enough to see Prophet Muhammad's mission, but he would not.

When the unbelievers were persecuting the Muslims in Makkah, Armah, the King of Ethiopia, offered to protect them. The king (called *Najashi* in Arabic) was a Christian, as were most people in his land. He said that he would defend any Muslim who came to live in his country from the *Kuffar*. Rasulullah ﷺ was very grateful to the king for this help.

Despite the fact that Muslims and Christians have fought each other at times throughout history, Muslims have a special relationship with them. Muslims and Christians share many beliefs. They both believe in One God; both believe in prophets, angels as well as life after death; they both also love and respect Jesus (`Isa ﷺ) and his mother Mary (Maryam ﷺ).

WE HAVE LEARNED
- The rapid spread of Islam alarmed the Roman Empire.
- Christianity and Islam have many points in common.
- The Qur'an describes Christians as being the closest to the believers.

WORDS TO KNOW
Embracing, Preachers, Bahira, Waraqa ibn Nawfil

QUR'AN CONNECTION

Allah ﷻ informed Muslims that despite differences in religion and culture, Christians have a special relationship with them:

وَلَتَجِدَنَّ أَقْرَبَهُم مَّوَدَّةً لِّلَّذِينَ ءَامَنُواْ ٱلَّذِينَ قَالُوٓاْ إِنَّا نَصَـٰرَىٰ ذَٰلِكَ بِأَنَّ مِنْهُمْ قِسِّيسِينَ وَرُهْبَانًا وَأَنَّهُمْ لَا يَسْتَكْبِرُونَ ﴿٨٢﴾

"And you will find the nearest in friendliness to those who believe those who say: 'Behold! We are Christians.' That is because there are among them priests and monks, and because they are not proud."

(al-Ma'idah 5:82)

Meeting the Roman Empire (2)

Looking Ahead

The Roman Empire decided to take action against the Muslims. Let's find out what steps were taken by Rasulullah ﷺ to protect the community.

Rasulullah ﷺ sent messengers to invite some of the Arab tribes that lived in the Roman Empire to Islam. When one Muslim preacher asked some of them to think about Islam, the people became angry and killed him. The Prophet ﷺ sent Zaid ibn Haritha ﷺ with an army of 3,000 men to punish those who had treacherously slain the preacher.

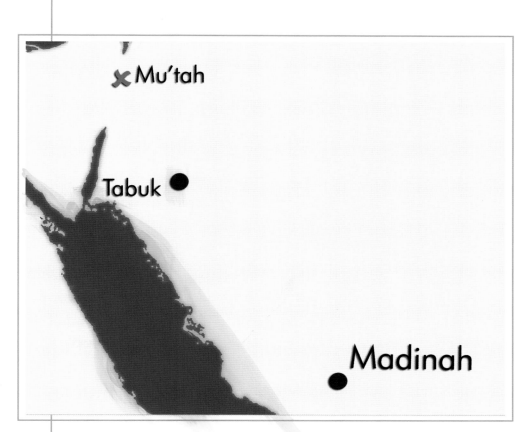

The Muslim army marched through the harsh desert lands north of Madinah to reach Tabuk and Mu'tah.

But the tribes called on the Roman army for protection. At a place called Mu'tah the Muslims met the Romans and their Arab allies. It was a terrible battle and many *Sahabah* fell. But the Muslims held their ground and the Romans withdrew.

The Roman Empire was very wealthy and powerful. Its generals gathered a huge army to attack Madinah. The Muslims would be no match for such an army. When Rasulullah heard word of the Roman plan, he decided to go north towards Syria to attack before the enemy could gather its strength. When the Muslims heard of Rasulullah's decision to do this they were puzzled. But they did not argue and said, "Allah and His Prophet know best. We shall obey and do what we are asked to do."

The *Munafiqun*, on the other hand, were frightened. They knew that fighting the Romans would mean certain defeat. They made up excuses to keep from going with the believers to battle. A few Muslims of weak faith also stayed behind, but most of the men obeyed the Prophet.

The Muslim army began their march in the middle of summer. The weather was extremely hot and the sun was scorching. Rasulullah was now sixty years old, but he decided to lead the army himself. Even though the Muslim army had over 30,000 men, any Roman army would be much, much larger.

After a long and tiring march through the desert, the Muslims reached a place called Tabuk. They waited many days for word of the enemy, but received none. In fact, the Roman army never came. Seeing as there was no army to battle, Rasulullah decided to call all of the local Arab chiefs together and invite them to Islam. Thus, the Muslims won a victory without fighting at all!

Rasulullah returned to Madinah from Tabuk satisfied. The Muslims who had not gone with the army now felt ashamed. They begged for Allah's forgiveness. Eventually Allah sent Rasulullah *Wahi* saying that He had forgiven them.

About this time, the leader of the *Munafiqun*, Ibn Ubai, passed away.

Rasulullah ﷺ led the funeral prayer over him and covered his body with his own shirt. Upon seeing Rasulullah's care for one of his worst enemies, many of the *Munafiqun* became true believers. Rasulullah ﷺ forgave all of them and prayed that Allah ﷻ would forgive them too.

As time went by more and more people wanted to know about Islam. Between the eighth and tenth years after the *Hijrah* many delegations came to Madinah to visit Rasulullah ﷺ and to accept Islam. Rasulullah ﷺ also sent many teachers to the tribes to invite them to Islam.

The *Ummah* of Muhammad ﷺ had now become the strongest power in Arabia. Allah ﷻ had fulfilled His Promises to the Muslims by granting them success in this life and the next.

WE HAVE LEARNED
- When a huge Roman Army was getting ready to attack Madinah, Rasulullah ﷺ marched to Tabuk with an army.
- The Muslims gained a victory at Tabuk without fighting. Many chiefs accepted Islam.
- Rasulullah ﷺ received many delegations and sent many preachers to spread Islam.

WORDS TO KNOW
Campaigns, Conqueror, Delegations, Freedom of Religion, Fullfil

QUR'AN CONNECTION
Allah ﷻ says about His promise to the believers,

وَنُرِيدُ أَن نَّمُنَّ عَلَى ٱلَّذِينَ ٱسۡتُضۡعِفُواْ فِي
ٱلۡأَرۡضِ وَنَجۡعَلَهُمۡ أَئِمَّةً وَنَجۡعَلَهُمُ ٱلۡوَٰرِثِينَ ۝

*"And We wanted to show Our Favor to those who were weak in the land,
and to make them the leaders and to make them the inheritors."*

(al-Qasas 28:5)

The Farewell Pilgrimage
(The 10th year of the *Hijrah*)

Looking Ahead

All of the Muslims gathered with Rasulullah ﷺ in Makkah to make *Hajj* one last time with him. Read the message he had to give them.

Rasulullah's mission in this world was now nearing its end. Twenty-three years had passed since Allah ﷻ sent the first revelations and now the Qur'an was almost complete. Most of the Arab tribes had entered Islam, and Islam had started to spread beyond the borders of Arabia. Allah ﷻ asked Rasulullah ﷺ to spend more time in prayer.

Rasulullah ﷺ desired to make the *Hajj* one last time. Most of the *Sahabah* wanted to go with him. News spread among the tribes and they came to join in the *Hajj* as well. When Rasulullah ﷺ entered Makkah there were about 12,000 Muslims with him. There were no enemies in sight. In fact, all of those who once opposed Islam had now become its devoted followers.

On the third day of the *Hajj*, the Muslims gathered on the Plain of Arafat. Rasulullah ﷺ stood on top of the hill called *Jabal ar-Rahmah*, the Mount of Mercy. There he made a

THINK ABOUT IT

In his farewell speech Rasulullah ﷺ said,"Be kind to your women."

Give one example of the unkindness of the Arabs before Islam towards their girls and women.

farewell sermon, the *Khutbah al-Wada'*, to the thousands of Muslims gathered. He said:

"Allah alone is worthy of praise. Fear Allah and obey Him.
Listen to what I say, for I may not be with you after this year.
If people give you a trust, keep their trust.
Respect the life, property, and honor of others.
One day you will go before Allah
and you will answer for all you have done.
Everyone is responsible for his own actions."

"All Muslims are brothers to one another.
Be kind to your women.
Obey your rulers and leaders as long as they obey Allah."

"I am leaving you the Qur'an and my Sunnah. Hold fast to these and you
will never go astray."

"O people! The pride in the days of Jahiliyyah has ended.
You are all children of Adam, and Adam was made of the dust.
Arabs and non-Arabs are all equal,
and the only thing that makes one person better than another
is the conciousness of Allah in his heart and his good deeds.

"O people, listen carefully to these words of mine."

Then Rasulullah ﷺ asked all those gathered, "Those of you who are present must give this message to those who are not." Allah ﷻ then sent *Wahi* telling Rasulullah ﷺ that:

$$\text{ٱلْيَوْمَ أَكْمَلْتُ لَكُمْ دِينَكُمْ وَأَتْمَمْتُ عَلَيْكُمْ}$$
$$\text{نِعْمَتِى وَرَضِيتُ لَكُمُ ٱلْإِسْلَـٰمَ دِينًا}$$

"This day I have perfected your religion for you and completed My favor upon
you, and have chosen Islam for your way of life."

(al-Ma'idah 5:3)

Many of the people gathered then realized that Rasulullah's mission had been fulfilled, and that the time for him to return to Allah ﷻ was near. The thought of this made them very sad.

WE HAVE LEARNED
- Rasulullah ﷺ made his "Farewell Pilgrimage" and most of the *Sahabah* accompanied him.
- Rasulullah ﷺ gave his last speech, the *Khutbah al-Wada'*, on the *Jabal ar-Rahmah*.
- *Wahi* informed Rasulullah ﷺ that the message of Islam had been completed.

WORDS TO KNOW
Devoted, Farewell, *Jabal ar-Rahmah*, *Khutbah al-Wada'*, Perfected

QUR'AN CONNECTION
Allah ﷻ says about the brotherhood of humankind,

$$يَـٰٓأَيُّهَا ٱلنَّاسُ إِنَّا خَلَقْنَـٰكُم مِّن ذَكَرٍ وَأُنثَىٰ وَجَعَلْنَـٰكُمْ شُعُوبًا$$

$$وَقَبَآئِلَ لِتَعَارَفُوٓا۟ إِنَّ أَكْرَمَكُمْ عِندَ ٱللَّهِ أَتْقَىٰكُمْ إِنَّ ٱللَّهَ عَلِيمٌ خَبِيرٌ ﴿١٣﴾$$

"O mankind! Indeed, We created you from a male and female, and made you into nations and tribes so that you might know one another.
Truly, the noblest of you in the Sight of Allah are the ones who are the most righteous. And Allah has full knowledge an is well acquainted with all things"

(al-Hujurat 49:13)

Lesson 18

The Last Journey of Rasulullah ﷺ

Looking Ahead

Allah has told us that everything that is born must one day die. We shall read how Rasulullah ﷺ and his community prepared for his leaving this life.

After returning from Makkah, Prophet Muhammad ﷺ spent more and more of his time in prayer. After a while he grew ill, but for a time he continued to lead *salat* in the *Masjid an-Nabi*. But when he became too weak, he asked his dear friend Abu Bakr ؓ to lead the prayers. His *Sahabah* continued to perform their *salat* in the *masjid*. Since they were used to seeing Rasulullah ﷺ five times a day, it made them very sad not to see him now.

Soon Rasulullah ﷺ was hardly able to stand. He made his *Salat* while he lay in his bed. He constantly prayed to Allah ﷻ that his *ummah* be granted blessings and forgiveness. He asked Allah ﷻ to save all human beings from the tricks and traps of *Shaitan*.

One day Rasulullah ﷺ arose from his bed. He went to the door of the *Masjid an-Nabi* and saw the Muslims making their *salat*. How pleased he was to see Allah's Commands being followed! There was a smile on his face when he returned to his bed.

He talked to his daughter, Fatimah ؓ, and his aunt, Safiyah ؓ. "Always do good to others, even if they harm you," he told them, "for only goodness will help you in the Hereafter." He asked his wife `A'ishah ؓ to give everything he had to the poor. "I leave behind only the Qur'an and my *Sunnah* to the world," he said.

From time to time he would fall unconscious, but when he recovered he kept saying, "Treat your servants and workers kindly. Always make your *Salat*."

Finally his time to depart came. As he took his last breath he said, "I go to the Best of Friends." And with that the beloved Prophet Muhammad ﷺ left this world. May Allah's peace and best blessings be upon him forever! *Amin!*

Rasulullah ﷺ brought us Islam. He gave us Allah's Word, the Qur'an. He was an example of a perfect human being. Rasulullah's conduct is our example that we must follow as truly as we can. Now that we know about the life of Prophet Muhammad ﷺ we should follow what Allah ﷻ tells us to do in the Qur'an along with following his example. We must also share the message of Rasulullah ﷺ with others.

After Rasulullah's death, the Muslims chose Abu Bakr ﷺ to be their leader. They called him the *Khalifat ur-Rasulullah*, the Successor of Rasulullah. The Muslim *Ummah* obeyed their new leader. They became united under their *Khalifah* to work to spread Islam.

After Rasulullah ﷺ left this world the Muslims went north toward the Roman Empire. They went south toward Yemen. They went east toward the Persia. They went west toward Egypt. They went everywhere it was possible to go. They worked hard for Islam, and soon Islam became one of the greatest religions in the world.

All praises are for Allah ﷻ, the Lord of the Worlds, and may His blessings and peace be on Muhammad ﷺ, the Most Noble Messenger and Best of Creation!

WE HAVE LEARNED
- When Rasulullah ﷺ became too sick to lead the *Salat*, he asked Abu Bakr ﷺ to lead.
- Before he died, he gave away all he had to the poor.
- He left the Qur'an and his *Sunnah* as a guide for everyone.

WORDS TO KNOW
Eternal, Example, Guide, *Khalifat ur-Rasulullah*

QUR'AN CONNECTION

In the Qur'an Allah ﷻ tells us about the importance of following the Prophet ﷺ,

مَّن يُطِعِ ٱلرَّسُولَ فَقَدْ أَطَاعَ ٱللَّهَ

"Whoever obeys Rasulullah certainly obeys Allah."

(an-Nisa' 4:80)

A Mercy to Mankind

Looking Ahead

As Rasulullah ﷺ was sent as a mercy from Allah ﷻ, so we Muslims must also reflect his mercy in our daily lives.

Mercy and compassion are very important human characteristics. These are the characteristics of Allah ﷻ, the Prophet Muhammad ﷺ and his *Ummah*. The Qur'an describes Allah ﷻ as the Most-Merciful (*ar-Rahman*) and Most-Compassionate (*ar-Rahim*).

In fact every *Surah* in the Qur'an (except one) starts with:

$$بِسْمِ ٱللَّهِ ٱلرَّحْمَـٰنِ ٱلرَّحِيمِ$$

"In the name of God Most Merciful and Most Compassionate."

Allah ﷻ has many beautiful names. But the names of His Mercy, *ar-Rahman* and *ar-Rahim*, are very important. The Qur'an says:

$$رَبَّنَا وَسِعْتَ كُلَّ شَيْءٍ رَّحْمَةً وَعِلْمًا فَٱغْفِرْ لِلَّذِينَ تَابُواْ$$
$$وَٱتَّبَعُواْ سَبِيلَكَ وَقِهِمْ عَذَابَ ٱلْجَحِيمِ$$

"O our Lord! You cover everything in Your Mercy and Knowledge. Forgive then those who repent and follow Your Path and protect them from the Hellfire."

(*al-Ghafir* 40:7)

Allah ﷻ has proven His Mercy to the universe by sending Rasulullah ﷺ for all of humankind to follow. The Qur'an says:

$$وَمَآ أَرْسَلْنَٰكَ إِلَّا رَحْمَةً لِّلْعَٰلَمِينَ ۝$$

"We have not sent you (O Muhammad) except as
a mercy for all the worlds."

(*al-Anbiya'* 21:107)

Allah ﷻ is Merciful towards us. Rasulullah ﷺ was merciful to all humanity. He had a special love and concern for his *Ummah*:

$$لَقَدْ جَآءَكُمْ رَسُولٌ مِّنْ أَنفُسِكُمْ عَزِيزٌ عَلَيْهِ$$
$$مَا عَنِتُّمْ حَرِيصٌ عَلَيْكُم بِٱلْمُؤْمِنِينَ رَءُوفٌ رَّحِيمٌ ۝$$

"There has come to you a Messenger from among yourselves,
grievous to him is your suffering, concerned for you; for the
believers full of compassion, merciful."

(*At-Tawbah* 9:128)

In fact, with one short sentence Rasulullah ﷺ summed up all the Islamic teachings about mercy:

"He who shows no mercy to others, Allah will show no mercy to him."

(*Bukhari, Muslim*)

Islam teaches us that all human beings are the creation of One God. The Qur'an and the *Sunnah* tell us that we are all children of Adam, and that Adam ﷺ was made of clay. Allah ﷻ tells us:

$$يَٰٓأَيُّهَا ٱلنَّاسُ إِنَّا خَلَقْنَٰكُم مِّن ذَكَرٍ وَأُنثَىٰ وَجَعَلْنَٰكُمْ شُعُوبًا$$
$$وَقَبَآئِلَ لِتَعَارَفُوٓا۟ إِنَّ أَكْرَمَكُمْ عِندَ ٱللَّهِ أَتْقَىٰكُمْ إِنَّ ٱللَّهَ عَلِيمٌ خَبِيرٌ ۝$$

Lesson 20

The *Sirah* of Rasulullah ﷺ:
A Perfect Life

Looking Ahead

We follow Rasulullah ﷺ because we know his life was perfect in every way. This is a special blessing that Allah had granted to him.

Let us now read about the aspects of the personality of Rasulullah ﷺ that made him such an important and unique person in history.

We have been blessed with the opportunity to study the *Sirah*. The *Sirah* is the biography of Rasulullah ﷺ. Allah ﷻ sent him to us as a true model to follow. Allah ﷻ says in the Qur'an:

لَّقَدْ كَانَ لَكُمْ فِى رَسُولِ ٱللَّهِ أُسْوَةٌ حَسَنَةٌ لِّمَن كَانَ يَرْجُوا۟ ٱللَّهَ وَٱلْيَوْمَ ٱلْأَخِرَ وَذَكَرَ ٱللَّهَ كَثِيرًا ﴿٢١﴾

"Indeed, you have in the Messenger of Allah an excellent example, for one who has hope in Allah and the Last Day, and who remembers Allah."

(al-Ahzab 33:21)

Islam teaches us that Allah ﷻ has sent many messengers and guides to teach humanity the way to True Faith. He sent these prophets as teachers to every nation and community. However, we know a little about a few of them and not much at all about most of them.

The life of Rasulullah ﷺ is unique in this respect. Unlike most of prophets throughout history, we know about the life and teachings of Muhammad ﷺ in great detail. This is because Allah ﷻ wants us to follow in his footsteps. His behavior is called *Uswah Hasanah*, the most beautiful of conduct.

The following are some unique aspects of the *Sirah* of Rasulullah ﷺ as explained by a well-known scholar, Syed Sulaiman Nadvi:

A PERFECT MODEL: The gentle character and attractive personality of the Prophet ﷺ and his clear thinking kept those around him inspired and committed. He motivated absolute devotion and respect in his followers during his lifetime, as he continues to do so even now. Nowhere in history is there another example of a leader who has so completely transformed the lives of his people, or been so deeply loved. Allah ﷻ says in the Qur'an:

$$\text{لَقَدْ مَنَّ ٱللَّهُ عَلَى ٱلْمُؤْمِنِينَ إِذْ بَعَثَ فِيهِمْ رَسُولاً مِّنْ أَنفُسِهِمْ}$$
$$\text{يَتْلُواْ عَلَيْهِمْ ءَايَـٰتِهِۦ وَيُزَكِّيهِمْ وَيُعَلِّمُهُمُ ٱلْكِتَـٰبَ وَٱلْحِكْمَةَ}$$

"Surely, Allah has given a favor to the believers when He raised among them a messenger from among themselves; he recites to them His Revelations and purifies them, and teaches them the Book and Wisdom."

(*Ali 'Imran*: 3:164)

Rasulullah ﷺ is the perfect example for us to follow if we want to lead a life full of spiritual meaning and worldly blessings.

AN IDEAL LIFE: Rasulullah ﷺ spent his life following the teachings of the Qur'an. He showed us how a true believer should live out his or her life. Muhammad ﷺ was a Prophet of Allah, a leader of an *Ummah*, a teacher and a family man. Rasulullah ﷺ taught us that we too could marry, raise a family and enjoy the good and *Halal* things of this life if we have the right intentions. Allah ﷻ rewards us for all of our actions if they are done with true intentions.

A HISTORIC LIFE: The life and teachings of the Prophet Muhammad ﷺ have been recorded in great detail by his *Sahabah*. He was not a legendary or mythical being. The accounts of Rasulullah's life have been derived from real sources and historical records. We know about all the daily aspects of the life of Muhammad Rasulullah ﷺ. He taught us how to live in wealth as well as in poverty. As a leader of a community and as a family man, he showed us how to behave in public and in private. All aspects of the life of Rasulullah ﷺ are practical and relevant for us to follow. History has completely recorded all aspects of his life.

THE MESSAGE AND ITS CONTINUITY: Allah ﷻ sent many prophets and messengers to humankind throughout history. Only few of them are still remembered and followed by the people. Islam is a living faith embraced by nearly one out of every five people on earth.

Rasulullah ﷺ prepared his *Sahabah* to carry his teachings to the newer generations. Early Muslims learned Islam through direct contact with these original sources. They practiced what they had learned and passed it on. Later generations carried these traditions until they came down to us.

WE HAVE LEARNED
- Rasulullah's life was unique in many ways and he was a "perfect model".
- Rasulullah ﷺ was real person in history who lived a practical life, putting his teachings into action.
- The message of Rasulullah ﷺ still continues after more than 1400 years.

WORDS TO KNOW
Unique, Perfect, Ideal, Historic, Continuity

HADITH CONNECTION
Rasulullah ﷺ said that we should always be aware of the actions we do:

"Should you want to do something, think about the consequences of doing it. If they are good, do it; if not, abstain from it."

(*Ibn al-Mubarak*)

The Unique Life of Rasulullah :
The Makkan Period

Looking Ahead

Do you remember the challenges that Rasulullah ﷺ and the Muslims faced while they were living in Makkah?

The Qur'an is the greatest miracle that was granted to Rasulullah ﷺ. Unlike many other ancient documents, the Qur'an has remained unchanged. What we read today in our *Masajid*, classrooms and homes is exactly what was given to Rasulullah ﷺ.

The preservation of the *Sunnah* of Rasulullah ﷺ (his life and teachings) is another marvel. The life of Rasulullah ﷺ can only be valued if we accept him for who he was: the Messenger of Allah. He received his guidance directly from Allah ﷻ.

Let us look at the distinctive features of Rasulullah's life in Makkah, where he spent his first fifty-three years. He became an orphan at an early age. He never went to school or learned how to read and write. The Qur'an describes the society he was born as *Ummiyyun*, an unlettered society. The Arabs at that time did not care much for reading and writing.

Throughout the world we can still see the remains of people gone by.

The Unique Life of Rasulullah ﷺ:
The Madinan Period

Looking Ahead

The migration to Madinah brought new challenges to the Muslim community. Rasulullah ﷺ laid the foundation of an ideal society based on Islamic principles.

Rasulullah's life in Madinah was the continuation of his mission in Makkah. In Makkah, Rasulullah ﷺ brought only few people to Islam. They became his devoted *Sahabah*. They lived and suffered in Makkah until Allah ﷻ gave them the orders to migrate to Madinah.

Rasulullah ﷺ faced the task of building a community with a handful of *Muhajirun* and the new Muslims of Madinah. This was a big challenge. Although Rasulullah ﷺ had the support and generosity of *Ansar*, not everyone living in Madinah was convinced of his mission or his intentions. He had to deal with a group called the *Munafiqun*, who openly accepted Islam, yet in private plotted against the Muslims. There were also three Jewish tribes who saw a threat in the growing strength of the Muslim community in Madinah.

For nearly seven years the Muslims of Madinah fought to defend themselves against those who sought to harm them. The three final years of Rasulullah's life were spent in *Da'wah*, liberating Makkah, and responding to the challenges from the Roman Empire far to the North.

In spite of all the hardships and sacrifices, Rasulullah ﷺ was not angry or bitter. He was no ordinary man. The Creator of the Universe guided him and he knew that all his actions were for a great mission. Rasulullah's final entry into Makkah after ten years of struggle was a unique victory that he credited to Allah ﷻ alone. He declared: "Allah alone has defeated His adversaries." He immediately forgave all those who fought against the Muslims, even those who were his worst enemies.

Armed struggle was part of the history of Muslims in Madinah, but it was only one part. Madinah became a polite society during the time of Rasulullah ﷺ. Feuds and quarrels were settled and people treated one another as brothers and sisters. *salah, sawm, zakat* and *hajj* were made obligatory for Muslims. Social, political, and business rules were put into practice. The *Shari`ah* started the standards of *halal* and *haram*.

The standards of a civilized society were defined by words of Allah and acted upon by Rasulullah ﷺ and his *Sahabah*. The Qur'anic terms of justice (`*Adl*) and equality (*Qist*) became the norms of an Islamic society.

Let us imagine how one human being, standing alone nearly twenty-three years, attacked and harassed by his own people, could have achieved so much? The Qur'an says:

إِنَّ ٱلَّذِينَ قَالُوا۟ رَبُّنَا ٱللَّهُ ثُمَّ ٱسْتَقَٰمُوا۟ تَتَنَزَّلُ عَلَيْهِمُ ٱلْمَلَٰٓئِكَةُ أَلَّا تَخَافُوا۟ وَلَا تَحْزَنُوا۟ وَأَبْشِرُوا۟ بِٱلْجَنَّةِ ٱلَّتِى كُنتُمْ تُوعَدُونَ ۝

"As for those who say: 'Our Lord is Allah', they are steadfast, the angels descend upon them saying, "Fear not nor grieve, but receive the good news of Jannah, That you were promised.""

(*Fussilat* 41:30)

One part of the way of life established by Rasulullah ﷺ was the freedom he gave to other religious traditions. No one was ever forced to give up his or her faith. The Qur'an tells the members of other religions to follow their own scriptures and to look for what they have in common with Muslims. Throughout history Muslims have respected the places of worship of Christians, Jews and others and guarded over their monasteries and libraries. This practice opened the doors for the participation of all citizens to live in a cooperative society.

WE HAVE LEARNED

- In Madinah, Rasulullah ﷺ faced the task of building a whole community.
- Rasulullah ﷺ protected the freedom and security of the people of other religions.
- Rasulullah ﷺ did not claim any credit for his success, but attributed everything to Allah ﷻ alone.

WORDS TO KNOW

'Adl, Monastery, *Qist*, *Shari`ah*

HADITH CONNECTION

It is important that we control our anger in every situation. Rasulullah ﷺ said:

"Allah hides the sins of the person who controls his or her anger."

(*Ibn Abi ad-Dunya*)

Lesson 23 A Teacher to Mankind

Looking Ahead

Let us think about all the wonderful ways that Rasulullah ﷺ taught us to become better human beings.

Once Rasulullah ﷺ was passing by a group of people as they were praying their *salat* and making many *du'as* to Allah ﷻ. He was pleased to see them doing this. He walked a little further and saw some other people engaged in teaching new Muslims about Islam. He was much more pleased to see this. He sat with these people and said, "Certainly, I have been sent as a teacher."

Allah ﷻ sent every prophet and messenger as a teacher to humankind. Rasulullah ﷺ came with the teachings of all the prophets in their perfection and completion. He is the highest of teachers. The Qur'an says about him:

كَمَآ أَرْسَلْنَا فِيكُمْ رَسُولاً مِّنكُمْ يَتْلُواْ عَلَيْكُمْ ءَايَٰتِنَا وَيُزَكِّيكُمْ وَيُعَلِّمُكُمُ ٱلْكِتَٰبَ وَٱلْحِكْمَةَ وَيُعَلِّمُكُم مَّا لَمْ تَكُونُواْ تَعْلَمُونَ ﴿١٥١﴾

"We have sent among you a messenger of your own, reciting to you Our Revelations, and purifying you, and teaching you the Book and Wisdom and that what you did not know."

(al-Baqarah 2:151)

IN THIS AYAH WE LEARN THAT:

● Rasulullah ﷺ was a human being like us. He was not an angel or some other supernatural being. Nevertheless, he was no ordinary human being. He is the Crown of Allah's creation, and the most perfect example of righteousness and goodness. Nothing in creation can ever come close to his level of excellence.

- Allah ﷻ revealed the Qur'an to Rasulullah ﷺ by way of Angel Jibril ﷺ. Rasulullah ﷺ taught his *Sahabah* the Qur'an. All the *ayat* of the Qur'an are Allah's signs. They show us the Knowledge, Power and Mercy of our Creator.

- Rasulullah ﷺ taught us how to purify and clean ourselves (*tazkiyyah*). Through the purification of our bodies, hearts and minds we can clean ourselves of bad thoughts and actions and become closer to Allah ﷻ. We can only do this by following Rasulullah's example.

- Rasulullah ﷺ taught us wisdom (*hikmah*). All his teachings have wisdom in them. Rasulullah's teachings are called the *Sunnah*. *Sunnah* means "The Way." True wisdom is to lead a life of faith, submitting to the Will of Allah ﷻ and following the example of Rasulullah ﷺ. This life actually prepares us for the life of the Hereafter, which lasts forever.

- Rasulullah ﷺ taught us about things that we did not know before. He informed us about the purpose of our existence. He gave us the insight to make our lives meaningful. He prepared us for the eternal life of the Hereafter.

- Rasulullah ﷺ was *Ummi*, yet had gained deep wisdom and knowledge directly from Allah ﷻ. He explained, "My Lord has taught me and that is the best of knowledge."

The teachings of the Qur'an and *Sunnah* cover all aspects of our lives. Allah ﷻ promised to protect His final revelation from change or corruption. It is the special favor of Allah that we have the Qur'an as well as the best of teachers to explain it. `A'ishah ﷺ, the wife of the Prophet, once said that Rasulullah's "character and personality was the Qur'an." He was a true teacher who practiced what he taught. In fact the Prophet Muhammad ﷺ is the perfect teacher for everyone and for all times to come.

WE HAVE LEARNED

- The teachings of the Qur'an and the *Sunnah* cover all aspects of our lives.
- Rasulullah ﷺ taught us those things that we did not know.
- Rasulullah ﷺ taught us *tazkiyah*, how to purify our hearts.

WORDS TO KNOW

Hikmah, Tazkiyah, Ummi

HADITH CONNECTION

Rasulullah ﷺ said:

"Always keep Allah in your mind wherever you are; follow a bad deed with a good one; and treat everyone politely."

(*at-Tirmidhi*)

The Qur'an:
The Greatest Miracle

Looking Ahead

Miracles are special acts performed on the command of Allah ﷻ that no other human can produce or imitate. Allah ﷻ gave miracles to the prophets as proof of their heavenly missions.

Allah ﷻ supported all the prophets by allowing them to perform special miracles. These miracles were special acts performed on the Command of Allah ﷻ. No ordinary human can produce or imitate these miracles.

Allah ﷻ blessed Rasulullah ﷺ with many miracles. He made the moon split into two, he caused a little food to feed many, and he made water appear from the palms of his hands. Yet his most important miracle was the Qur'an. This is a miracle that will last through time and will always witness to the truth of his mission.

The Qur'an is the greatest book of wisdom and guidance given to humankind. It was revealed to a prophet who did not know how to read or write. The Qur'an challenges those who have doubts about its authenticity:

The Miracles of the Prophet ﷺ

'Abdullah ibn Mas'ud ﷺ said, "We were with Rasulullah ﷺ at Mina when the moon was split in two. One of its parts was behind this mountain and the other one behind that mountain. Rasulullah ﷺ said to us, 'Bear witness to this.'" - *Sahih Muslim*

Anas ﷺ said, "Once during the lifetime of Rasulullah ﷺ, the people of Madinah suffered from a drought. So while the Prophet was delivering a *Khutbah* on a Friday a man got up saying, 'O Rasulullah! The horses and sheep have perished. Will you pray to God to bless us with rain?' The Prophet lifted both his hands and prayed. The sky at that time was as clear as glass. Suddenly a wind blew, raising clouds that gathered together, and it started raining heavily. We came out of the *Masjid* wading through the flooding water till we reached our homes. It went on raining till the next Friday, when the same man (or some other man) stood up and said, "O Rasulullah! The houses have collapsed; please pray for the rain to stop!" On that the Prophet smiled and said, 'O Allah! Let it rain around us and not on us.' I then looked at the clouds to see them separating, forming a sort of a crown round Madinah."- *Sahih ul-Bukhari*

قُل لَّئِنِ ٱجْتَمَعَتِ ٱلْإِنسُ وَٱلْجِنُّ عَلَىٰٓ أَن يَأْتُوا۟ بِمِثْلِ هَـٰذَا ٱلْقُرْءَانِ لَا يَأْتُونَ بِمِثْلِهِۦ وَلَوْ كَانَ بَعْضُهُمْ لِبَعْضٍ ظَهِيرًا ۝

"Say! Certainly, if all of humankind and the jinns were to gather together to produce the like of this Qur'an, they could not produce it, even if they support and help each other."

(al-Isra' 17:88)

The Qur'an is the very Word of Allah. It was revealed to Rasulullah ﷺ over a period of 23 years. It was revealed for 13 years in Makkah and then 10 years in Madinah.

The Qur'an guided Rasulullah ﷺ through his mission at every step. It contains the eternal message that Allah ﷻ sent to all the prophets and messengers before Rasulullah ﷺ. The Qur'an confirms what was given to Nuh, Ibrahim, Musa, Dawud, and `Isa ﷺ.

Allah ﷻ has safeguarded His Book just as He had promised. He shall continue to safeguard it. The Qur'an states:

إِنَّا نَحْنُ نَزَّلْنَا ٱلذِّكْرَ وَإِنَّا لَهُۥ لَحَـٰفِظُونَ ۝

"Indeed we have revealed this message and We shall safeguard it."

(al-Hijr 15:9)

LET US FIND OUT IN WHAT WAYS ALLAH ﷻ HAS SAFEGUARDED THE QUR'AN:

- First of all the words of the Qur'an are the precise words of Allah as they were revealed to the Prophet Muhammad ﷺ. From the time of its revelation until now, thousands upon thousands of individuals have memorized the entire Qur'an without a mistake from beginning to end. These people are called *huffaz* (singular, *hafiz*).

- There have been special people throughout history, called *muqris* or *qaris*, who recited the Qur'an exactly as Rasulullah ﷺ and his *Sahabah* recited it. These people exist today.

- Allah gave complete knowledge of the Qur'an to Rasulullah ﷺ. His *Sunnah* and his *Sirah* have been preserved so that they can explain the Qur'an and we can put its commands into practice.

- Allah ﷻ preserved Arabic, which is the language of the Qur'an. The Arabic language of the Qur'an is a living language, spoken, studied and understood by countless numbers of people today.

- A number of the *Sahabah* learned the meaning of the Qur'an as well as the occasion for the revelation of each and every *ayah*. This knowledge has been kept in books of explaining the Qur'an called *tafsir*. Consequently, Qur'anic words, expressions and meanings are now safeguarded in the books of *tafsir*.

Most important of all, Allah ﷻ has preserved knowledge of the Qur'an through a chain of *'ulama*, or scholars, stretching through the centuries. These *'ulama* spent their lives reading, understanding and practicing the Qur'an. Many of them founded schools where Islamic knowledge was taught.

Indeed! The Qur'an is a miracle of excellence and perfection in its language and content. Its preservation is also a unique miracle of Allah ﷻ, Who promised to preserve this last divine message in its original pure form.

WE HAVE LEARNED
- The Qur'an is a word for word revelation from Allah ﷻ.
- Allah ﷻ has safeguarded the Qur'an from any corruption just as He had promised.
- The Qur'an affirms all the messages sent to earlier prophets ﷺ.

WORDS TO KNOW
Divine, *Huffaz, Muqri, Qari, Tafsir, 'Ulama*

HADITH CONNECTION
Rasulullah ﷺ told us about the importance of reciting the Qur'an:

"The one who recites the Qur'an and then asks Allah for something,
a thousand angels say 'Amin.'"
(*al-Darimi*)

Lesson 25

The Miracle of the *Sunnah*

Looking Ahead

If we truly want to live our lives in the way of the Prophet ﷺ we have to be sure to follow his *Sunnah*.

We have discussed in the previous lesson how Rasulullah ﷺ received two unique miracles:

* **The Qur'an**
* **The *Sunnah***

Islam is the final religion from Allah ﷻ, and Muhammad ﷺ is His last prophet and messenger. Allah has promised to safeguard the Qur'an from changes and corruptions. We have seen how Allah ﷻ safeguards His Book. Let us see how the miracle of the *Sunnah* explains and preserves the Qur'an.

As we read before, `A'ishah ﷂ was once asked about the personality of Rasulullah ﷺ. She responded by saying that "His character was the Qur'an." The words of `A'ishah ﷂ tell us that the teachings of the Qur'an were put into practice with perfection by Rasulullah ﷺ. He was the Qur'an in action. It is important for Muslims to follow the teachings of Rasulullah ﷺ. Allah ﷻ tells the Prophet ﷺ to say to the believers:

قُلْ إِن كُنتُمْ تُحِبُّونَ ٱللَّهَ فَٱتَّبِعُونِى يُحْبِبْكُمُ ٱللَّهُ وَيَغْفِرْ لَكُمْ ذُنُوبَكُمْ ۚ وَٱللَّهُ غَفُورٌ رَّحِيمٌ ﴿٣١﴾

"If you love Allah, follow me; Allah will love you and forgive your sins. For Allah is Oft-Forgiving and Merciful"

(*Ali Imran 3:31*)

The above *ayah* tells us how important it is to follow the Prophet ﷺ. It is only through Rasulullah ﷺ that we have received the Qur'an. It is only through his *Sunnah* that we can understand the Qur'an.

The word *Sunnah* means the "Way" and "Practice". The *Sunnah* of Rasulullah covers three things:

* His words and teachings,
* His own actions and behavior,
* The actions that others did that he approved.

The *Sahabah* and later generations wrote down everything regarding Rasulullah's teachings as well as the details of his life. Rasulullah's teachings and actions are his *Sunnah*, his "Path." His teachings written down are called *Hadith*. The word *Hadith* literally means "story" or "speech". It also means something new or recent. However, nowadays when we use the word *Hadith*, it means the teachings, sayings and approval of things by Rasulullah ﷺ.

The *Hadith* and the *Sunnah* are basically the same. We can simply say that the practice of Rasulullah ﷺ is the *Sunnah* and its collected record is the *Hadith*. The *Hadith* is only next to the Qur'an in its importance. It is the second most important source of the *Shari'ah* (Islamic law). The *Hadith* is also inspired by Allah ﷻ. However, it is not as authentic as the Qur'an. If the Qur'an is the word of Allah ﷻ, the *Hadith* is its explanation by Rasulullah ﷺ.

The Qur'an is called *Wahi Matlu*. This means it is a revelation that is recited. *Hadith* is called *Wahi Ghair Matlu*. This means it is a revelation that is not recited. However, the scholars of Islam carefully studied both Qur'an and *Hadith*. Earlier generations of Muslims collected the *Sunnah* and compiled them into books of *Hadith*. Later generations continued to study these works and kept that knowledge fresh. They also added commentaries on the *Ahadith*. A scholar of *Hadith* is called a *muhaddith*. To be a *muhaddith* requires great study, knowledge and skill.

There are many books containing *Hadith*, but all of them are not ranked the same. Also, all *Ahadith* are not equally reliable. There are degrees of reliability with *Hadith*.

Each Hadith is divided into two parts:

1. **Isnad:** the chain of people who narrated it from the Prophet ﷺ.
2. **Matn:** the basic text of the *Hadith*.

The *Sahabah* were the first generation to receive Allah's message from Rasulullah ﷺ and then preserve it. The *Sahabah* themselves were excellent role models of goodness and belief. They transmitted Rasulullah's message to future generations. They also showed how to practice Islam in daily life. The connection continued on through the *'ulama*, the scholars of Islam. The Qur'an and the *Sunnah* are the miracles sent to light up the hearts of believers for all the generations to come.

WE HAVE LEARNED
- The teachings of the Qur'an were practiced with perfection by Rasulullah ﷺ.
- The *Hadith* are next to the Qur'an in importance for Muslims.
- The *Sahabah* transmitted Rasulullah's message to future generations of Muslims.

WORDS TO KNOW
Isnad, Matn, Muhaddith, Transmit, *Wahi Matlu, Wahi Ghair Matlu*

HADITH CONNECTION
Rasulullah ﷺ said:

> *"Covering peoples' mistakes is like bringing the dead back to life."*
>
> (*at-Tabarani*)

Looking Ahead

We all make promises to people all the time. As Muslims we should always fulfill our promises.

Allah ﷻ has told us in the Qur'an that we must fulfill our promises as well as honor our agreements and contracts with other people. The Qur'an teaches us that we must fulfill our promises, contracts and treaties faithfully:

وَأَوْفُواْ بِعَهْدِ ٱللَّهِ إِذَا عَٰهَدتُّمْ وَلَا تَنقُضُواْ ٱلْأَيْمَٰنَ بَعْدَ تَوْكِيدِهَا وَقَدْ جَعَلْتُمُ ٱللَّهَ عَلَيْكُمْ كَفِيلًا إِنَّ ٱللَّهَ يَعْلَمُ مَا تَفْعَلُونَ ﴿٩١﴾

"And fulfill the Covenant of Allah when you entered into it, and break not your oaths you have pledged them. Indeed you have made Allah as your witness; surely Allah knows what you do."

(An-Nahl 50:91)

Rasulullah ﷺ stood firm in fulfilling his promises and honoring the agreements and the treatise he made with others. It was because of this good characteristic that he was known as *as-Sadiq* (the Truthful) and *al-Amin* (the Trustworthy).

On one occasion a man promised to meet with Rasulullah ﷺ at a certain place. Rasulullah ﷺ went to that place at the agreed upon time and waited for that man. The man didn't show up but Rasulullah ﷺ waited there for several days. When the man remembered his promise, he ran to where Rasulullah ﷺ was waiting for him and begged for his forgiveness.

People in Makkah used to trust Rasulullah ﷺ and give him their precious belongings for safekeeping as an *amana*. Rasulullah ﷺ made a special effort to return all of this *amana* before he made *Hijrah*. He told `Ali ﷺ to remain in Makkah to make sure everything was given back to its rightful owner.

As leader of Madinah, Rasulullah ﷺ made agreements and treaties with Muslims and non-Muslims alike. He never broke those agreements and always kept his word. The Treaty of Hudaibiyah is a good example of his respect for treaties. When the position of Muslims was strong he entered into this treaty with the *Kuffar* and sacrificed many rights.

Rasulullah ﷺ signed treaties with many non-Muslim tribes and always honored them. Through those treaties, he granted social and religious rights to everyone. He set an example for his successors to respect the rights of non-Muslim communities that may be under their rule.

This became an example for future rulers as well. Following the model of Rasulullah ﷺ, later Muslims rulers, on the whole, treated the non-Muslim citizens of their lands with great tolerance and justice. Many non-Muslim actually left their lands to live under Muslim rule. For instance, when the king and queen of Spain expelled all of their Jewish subjects in the 15th century, most found safety in Muslim lands. They settled in Muslim cities like Istanbul, Sarajevo, Cairo and Salonika. In many ways, they too contributed to the development of Islamic civilization.

WE HAVE LEARNED
- Qur'an teaches us that we should always fulfill our promises, agreements and treaties.
- Rasulullah ﷺ set an example for us in fulfilling his promises.
- We should always follow the example of Rasulullah ﷺ in our relationships to all human beings, Muslims and non Muslims alike.

WORDS TO KNOW
Agreement, *Amana*, Civilization, Safekeeping, Refuge

HADITH CONNECTION
Rasulullah ﷺ said:

"Make thing easy, and do not make things difficult. Give encouraging words to people and do not make them run away from you."

(*Bukhari*)

Lesson 27

Justice:
A Characteristic of Rasulullah ﷺ

Looking Ahead

Do you know the oath a judge has to take?

Every civilized nation has established systems of justice. Justice occupies a very important place in Islamic teachings as well. The Qur'an uses two terms for justice: `Adl and Qist. Both mean justice, fairness, and equity. Total justice is a quality of Allah ﷻ alone. One of His Names is al-`Adil, the Just. But justice can be reflected in our lives. Allah ﷻ says in the Qur'an:

يَٰٓأَيُّهَا ٱلَّذِينَ ءَامَنُواْ كُونُواْ قَوَّٰمِينَ لِلَّهِ شُهَدَآءَ بِٱلۡقِسۡطِ وَلَا يَجۡرِمَنَّكُمۡ شَنَئَانُ قَوۡمٍ عَلَىٰٓ أَلَّا تَعۡدِلُواْ ٱعۡدِلُواْ هُوَ أَقۡرَبُ لِلتَّقۡوَىٰ وَٱتَّقُواْ ٱللَّهَ إِنَّ ٱللَّهَ خَبِيرُۢ بِمَا تَعۡمَلُونَ ۝

"O believers! Stand firmly for Allah as a witness to fairness and let not the hatred of others turn you away from doing justice. Be just, for that is next to piety, and be conciouss of Allah, for Allah knows well what you do."

(al-Ma'idah 5:8)

A noble characteristic of Rasulullah ﷺ was his justice. Another special quality of his was fairness. In Makkah he was known for his fairness, trust, mercy, and sincerity. He always settled disputes between people with patience and justice, like he did when he was a youth helping the quarreling Makkan tribes placing al-*Hajar al-Aswad* in its place. He settled the problem and made every one happy.

The most important characteristic Rasulullah ﷺ needed as a ruler was justice. There are three factors that contributed to this characteristic:

1. The Qur'an was a guide to justice for all, and it was fair and open.
2. Rasulullah ﷺ gave equal justice to all parties, Muslim and non-Muslim alike.
3. Rasulullah ﷺ had shown complete mercy in his private affairs and full justice in public affairs.

As the leader of Madinah and head of the *Ummah*, Rasulullah ﷺ had to solve and settle many disputes. He always made his decisions based on the Qur'an and, if need be, *Shura*.

WE HAVE LEARNED
- Justice is one of the most important Islamic teachings.
- Rasulullah ﷺ was a just and fair ruler in dealing with both Muslims and non-Muslims.
- All his decisions were made with mercy and justice.

WORDS TO KNOW
'Adl, 'Adil, Equity, *al-Hajar al-Aswad,* Justice

HADITH CONNECTION
It is important to be just at all times, even if it is hard to do. Rasulullah ﷺ said:

"Speak the Truth, even if it is unpleasant."

(Ibn Hibban)

Looking Ahead

Muslims are part of the human family. Allah ﷻ commands us to treat everyone with fairness and justice

Islam is the final religion revealed by Allah ﷻ. It is not really a new religion but it contains the message of all the prophets throughout time, which is basically to believe in One God, doing good and preventing evil. Islam is the conclusion of all the messages that have come to mankind and that can be found in most of the world's religions.

Force in religious matters is not allowed by the Qur'an or by the *Sunnah*. In fact it is a fundamental Islamic principle that individuals must be allowed to choose their own belief. Allah ﷻ says:

$$لَآ إِكْرَاهَ فِى ٱلدِّينِ$$

"There is no compulsion in religion"
(al-Baqarah 2:256)

The Qur'an tells us that Muslims are to invite people to Islam with wisdom and good advice. We must remember that "guidance is in the Hands of Allah Himself" (*al-Baqarah* 2:120). Any act of a Muslim that contradicts this teaching, such as threatening or forcing people to embrace Islam, is not acceptable to Allah ﷻ.

The Qur'an points out that there is a large variety of religions in the world. It accepts this diversity, and commands people to build relationships based on what they have in common, for instance the worship of One God (*Ali 'Imran*: 3:64). While the Qur'an acknowledges religious diversity, it shows that Muslims have special bonds with Jews and Christians, who are called "People of the Book." The Qur'an commands Muslims to discuss religious issues with the People of the Book in a polite and courteous way:

وَلَا تُجَـٰدِلُوٓا۟ أَهْلَ ٱلْكِتَـٰبِ إِلَّا بِٱلَّتِى هِىَ أَحْسَنُ

*"Do not enter into discussion with the People of the Book
except in a nice way..."*

(al-`Ankabut 29:46)

It is important for us to be polite when we talk to anyone, especially people of other faiths. We must appreciate what we have in common with other people. Although the above *ayah* refers to talks with the People of the Book, this basic principal applies to the followers of all of the world's religions. Allah ﷻ commands Muslims to find ways for living together. Islam teaches us that communication and discussion are necessary for making a peaceful and just society.

Rasulullah ﷺ was tolerant to every one. It was because of his love, kindness and generosity that most of the Arab tribes accepted Islam. The Qur'an makes this point very clear in the following *ayah*:

لَّا يَنْهَىٰكُمُ ٱللَّهُ عَنِ ٱلَّذِينَ لَمْ يُقَـٰتِلُوكُمْ فِى ٱلدِّينِ
وَلَمْ يُخْرِجُوكُم مِّن دِيَـٰرِكُمْ أَن تَبَرُّوهُمْ وَتُقْسِطُوٓا۟ إِلَيْهِمْ
إِنَّ ٱللَّهَ يُحِبُّ ٱلْمُقْسِطِينَ ۞

*"Allah does not forbid you to show goodness and practice justice
with those who do not fight your faith nor drive you from your homes.
Allah loves those who are just."*

(al-Mumtahinah 60:8)

It is important for Muslims to be respectful and fair towards every human being regardless of their race, religion, gender or nationality. The Qur'anic idea of justice does not discriminate between people. Muslims are a part of the larger human society. There are many countries where Muslims live as majority and many others where they are minorities.

The Qur'an and the *Sunnah* guide us in both situations commanding us to help build a peaceful and just society. Each Friday prayer sermon ends with a command from the Qur'an:

$$\text{إِنَّ ٱللَّهَ يَأْمُرُ بِٱلْعَدْلِ وَٱلْإِحْسَـٰنِ وَإِيتَآيِ ٱلْقُرْبَىٰ وَيَنْهَىٰ}$$

$$\text{عَنِ ٱلْفَحْشَآءِ وَٱلْمُنكَرِ وَٱلْبَغْيِ ۚ يَعِظُكُمْ لَعَلَّكُمْ تَذَكَّرُونَ ۝}$$

"Allah commands you to practice justice, to do good, and fulfill your duties to your relatives. He forbids you from rude actions, evil and injustice. Allah is telling you, so that you are reminded."
(*an-Nahl* 16:90)

This *ayah* sums up the true message of the Qur'an and the *Sirah* of Rasulullah ﷺ. It reminds us to use these teachings in our dealings with all people.

WE HAVE LEARNED
- Islam is not a new religion but it is a continuation of all the religions that human beings had received from the beginning of time.
- Muslims are a part of the larger human society.
- The Qur'an and the *Sunnah* enjoin upon Muslims to help build a just and peaceful world.

WORDS TO KNOW
Birr, Diversity, Justice, *Qist*

HADITH CONNECTION
Rasulullah ﷺ told us that we must do good to all. Then we will be high in the Sight of Allah ﷻ:

"The best of friends in the Sight of Allah is the person who is good to his friends; and the best neighbor in the Sight of Allah is the one who is good to his neighbors."
(*at-Tirmidhi*)

In the Footsteps of Rasulullah ﷺ

Looking Ahead

It is important that we reflect the true teachings of Rasulullah ﷺ. Our behavior can be the best way to teach others about Islam.

In his final days, Rasulullah ﷺ advised his *Ummah*:

"I am leaving for you two things: the Qur'an and my *Sunnah*. If you follow them you will be guided." *(Bukhari)*

This advice of Rasulullah ﷺ has the aid of Allah's promise to protect the Qur'an as well as the *Sunnah* of His Messenger. Allah ﷻ fulfills His promise by choosing certain people to fulfill His purpose. How fortunate are the people whom Allah ﷻ has chosen to support His Will!

Every Muslim has a responsibility to live the message of Islam and pass on this message to others. The Qur'an and the *Sunnah* are perfect guides for us to follow. In addition, we have the noble examples of the *Sahabah* and the righteous men and women who came after them. The Qur'an teaches us to:

$$ٱدْعُ إِلَىٰ سَبِيلِ رَبِّكَ بِٱلْحِكْمَةِ وَٱلْمَوْعِظَةِ ٱلْحَسَنَةِ ۖ وَجَٰدِلْهُم بِٱلَّتِى هِىَ أَحْسَنُ$$

"Invite people to the path of your Lord with wisdom and good advice and discuss with them in the best manner."
(*an-Nahl* 16:125)

This means that we:

1. Must give the message of Islam with wisdom and in a pleasing manner.
2. Discuss religious matters with others in a respectful and polite way.

True *Da`wah* (calling people to Islam) is not preaching, but it is practicing what we believe. If we behave in a good way, people will become impressed with us and we will be a good reflection of a true Muslim. We could preach all day about Islam, but if our behavior is incorrect, our words will have little positive effect on those around us. Allah ﷻ warns us against not acting on what we preach:

$$يَٰٓأَيُّهَا ٱلَّذِينَ ءَامَنُواْ لِمَ تَقُولُونَ مَا لَا تَفْعَلُونَ ۝$$

$$كَبُرَ مَقْتًا عِندَ ٱللَّهِ أَن تَقُولُواْ مَا لَا تَفْعَلُونَ ۝$$

"O you who believe! Why do you say that which you don't do yourself? It is the most disliked in the sight of Allah that you say what you don't do."

(as-Saffat 61:2-3)

Remember! Muslims are not a privileged group of people who can do whatever they please. The *Ummah* of Muhammad ﷺ is a responsible community. We have to fulfill our duties in relation to our families, communities, neighborhoods and our nation.

Islam is not a new religion. It started with Prophet Adam ﷺ and it continued on through a long line of prophets and messengers, a line finishing with Prophet Muhammad ﷺ. It is part of Muslim faith to believe in all the prophets and send salutations on them all.

As Muslims we must participate in all the things which are good and helpful to people, Muslim and non-Muslim alike. Along with our neighbors and fellow citizens we must oppose what is wrong. Allah ﷻ says:

$$وَتَعَاوَنُواْ عَلَى ٱلْبِرِّ وَٱلتَّقْوَىٰ وَلَا تَعَاوَنُواْ عَلَى ٱلْإِثْمِ وَٱلْعُدْوَٰنِ$$

"Cooperate in what is Just and righteous and do not cooperate in what is sinful and treacherous."

(al-Ma'idah 5: 2)

In our lives we shall certainly experience both good and bad things. But we have to remember that the Qur'an and the *Sunnah* command us to return whatever good someone has done to us only with good:

$$هَلْ جَزَآءُ ٱلْإِحْسَـٰنِ إِلَّا ٱلْإِحْسَـٰنُ ۝$$

"Is there a reward of a good deed other than a good deed?"
(ar-Rahman 55:60)

However returning evil with good is an even better act that will be greatly rewarded by Allah ﷾. In his life Rasulullah ﷺ set an example of how to return evil with good. The Qur'an tells us:

$$وَلَا تَسْتَوِى ٱلْحَسَنَةُ وَلَا ٱلسَّيِّئَةُ ۚ ٱدْفَعْ بِٱلَّتِى هِىَ أَحْسَنُ$$
$$فَإِذَا ٱلَّذِى بَيْنَكَ وَبَيْنَهُ عَدَٰوَةٌ كَأَنَّهُ وَلِىٌّ حَمِيمٌ ۝$$

"Goodness and evil cannot be equal. Push away evil with something which is good: You will see that he with whom you had enmity, will become your close friend."
(*Fussilat* 41:34)

Today Muslims live as majorities in nearly fifty countries. The laws of Islam state that all non-Muslims living in Muslim lands have to be respected. In the past Christians, Jews, Hindus and Buddhists who lived under Muslim rule generally did so in peace and harmony. We must always remember to follow the loving example of our Messenger, Muhammad ﷺ, a man who treated everyone with respect regardless of their faith.

Almost a third of the world's 1.4 billion Muslims live in nations where non-Muslims are a majority. In most modern countries laws declare that all of its citizens as equal. In many countries of the world we have democracy and pluralism. If we live in such countries, we must participate in all aspects of life with our fellow citizens to build healthy and prosperous nations. We must never engage in behavior that causes pain and loss to our neighbors and fellow citizens.

We must remember that Rasulullah ﷺ once said:

"A Muslim is one from whose hands and tongue people are safe."
(at-Tirmidhi)

It also means that we, as Muslims, must do every thing to make our societies a safe place for everyone. Then others will see the beauty of Islam reflected in our good actions.

WE HAVE LEARNED
- Muslims must participate in all the things which are good and helpful to people.
- The Qur'an and *Sunnah* tell us to return whatever good someone has done to us only with good.
- True *Da`wah* is not just preaching to others, but being a good example as well.

WORDS TO KNOW
Da`wah, Democracy, Intolerance, Participate, Pluralism

HADITH CONNECTION
Rasulullah ﷺ said:

*If you see something evil you should correct it with your hand,
and if that is not possible, correct it with your tongue,
and if that is not possible, you should hate it in your heart -
and that is the weakest (form) of faith.*
(Muslim)

"A Mercy for all the Worlds.."

Looking Ahead

The Prophet Muhammad ﷺ is a blessing for all of us. Let's read about his role in spreading the Mercy of Allah ﷻ.

The Qur'an says about Rasulullah ﷺ:

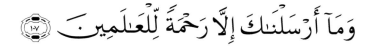

"We have not sent you except as a mercy for all the Worlds."

(al-Anbiya' 21:107)

Rasulullah ﷺ himself is a true model of the Mercy of Allah; he practiced himself what he taught others. His mercy extends to all humanity and to everything that Allah ﷻ created. Indeed Allah ﷻ had given Rasulullah ﷺ a very kind heart. The Qur'an says:

وَلَوۡ كُنتَ فَظًّا غَلِيظَ ٱلۡقَلۡبِ لَٱنفَضُّواْ مِنۡ حَوۡلِكَ ۖ
فَٱعۡفُ عَنۡهُمۡ وَٱسۡتَغۡفِرۡ لَهُمۡ وَشَاوِرۡهُمۡ فِي ٱلۡأَمۡرِ ۖ

"It is the Mercy of Allah that you are kind to them; if you were harsh, they would have left you. So overlook their mistakes, ask for Allah's forgiveness for them, and consult them in your affairs."

(Ali `Imran 3:159)

Rasulullah's kindness and compassion attracted people to him. Most of the people who met him believed in him and became faithful *Sahabah*. Even before he became a prophet he was well-known for his honesty, good character and kindness. When Allah ﷻ honored him with revelation, he was given a very special mission to perform. Love and mercy always guided this mission.

For thirteen years he preached in Makkah where he faced harsh opposition. He was tormented, made fun of and laughed at, but he never complained. He never felt hatred towards those who hated him. In his personal life he showed kindness to orphans, and care for the poor. He also protected widows and tried his best to free slaves.

Allah ﷻ made him head of a new community in Madinah. Most of the people of Madinah accepted Islam. He always used his power in the most thoughtful manner. He combined justice with mercy. He cared about all the people of Madinah, not just the Muslims. He was considerate to all his neighbors, many of whom were Jewish. He treated prisoners of war with respect and dignity. He even released all the prisoners of the Battle of Badr and forgave the prisoners of the Battle of Hunain and returned all their property to them.

Rasulullah ﷺ loved peace and did not like war. But three times the *Kuffar* attacked Madinah and he had no option but to defend his city by force. He set rules of wars by which women, children, the elderly and priests must not be harmed. He forbade destruction of all places of worship as well as the uprooting of vegetation and trees.

When Rasulullah ﷺ returned to Makkah eight years after the *Hijrah,* he showed exceptional mercy towards those who opposed him. He forgave all the *Kuffar.* He did not even allow the *Muhajirun* to reclaim their stolen property.

In addition to people, Rasulullah ﷺ taught us to be kind to all creatures. Tame animals must be fed properly, used carefully and loaded lightly. He forbade games in which animals fought, injured and often killed each other. He told us that if we have to kill an animal we must do so in the least painful way. In fact, he told us that causing pain on other creatures is wrong.

Rasulullah ﷺ forbade cutting the trees and destroying vegetation without a reason. Even during the wars he instructed safeguarding plants and trees. He encouraged cultivation and plantation. He said,

"If some one has a sapling in hand to plant and he discovers the Day of Judgment is only a day away, he must still plant."

(*Abu Dawud*)

He encouraged us to use water carefully. He advised not to waste food. He taught that we should share the resources of the earth so that our communities grow strong and happy. He said,

"When we share, the food of two is enough for three and food of three is enough for four."

(*al-Muwatta*)

He brought the *Shari`ah*, a law, which treats all human beings equally. The Qur'an teaches us to cooperate with others to build a better society.

وَتَعَاوَنُوا۟ عَلَى ٱلْبِرِّ وَٱلتَّقْوَىٰ ۖ وَلَا تَعَاوَنُوا۟ عَلَى ٱلْإِثْمِ وَٱلْعُدْوَٰنِ

"And cooperate with each other in doing good
and do not cooperate with each other in sin and transgression."

(*al-Ma'idah 5:2*)

WE HAVE LEARNED
- Rasulullah ﷺ was a true model of the Mercy of Allah.
- Rasulullah ﷺ always used his power in the most thoughtful manner.
- Islam gives us rules by which we must treat other people, animals and the environment.

WORDS TO KNOW
Compassion, Considerate, Exceptional, Torment

HADITH CONNECTION

Rasulullah ﷺ said:

"The Merciful One shows mercy to those who are themselves merciful to others. So show mercy to whatever is on earth, so that Allah will show mercy to you."

(*Abu Dawud, Tirmidhi*)